Beauty
in the
Brokenness

Beauty
in the
Brokenness

ONE WOMAN'S VOICE

Dr. Angela Lindenmuth Marick

BALBOA.
PRESS

A DIVISION OF HAY HOUSE

Balboa Press books may be ordered through booksellers or by contacting:

Balboa Press
A Division of Hay House
1663 Liberty Drive
Bloomington, IN 47403
www.balboapress.com
1 (877) 407-4847

Cover: The park in York, Pennsylvania, where we placed
Josh's special commemorative bench.
Frontispiece: Our family of four, April 2016.

Print information available on the last page.

ISBN: 978-1-9822-0532-4 (sc)
ISBN: 978-1-9822-0534-8 (hc)
ISBN: 978-1-9822-0533-1 (e)

Library of Congress Control Number: 2018906499

I dedicate this book to Joshua Andrew Lindenmuth, an extraordinary man, and our two precious boys, Justin and Carter.

(1975–2016)

"For God so loved the world that he gave his one and only Son, that whoever believes in him shall not perish but have eternal life." John 3:16

Contents

Preface

In July 2015, my husband, Josh Lindenmuth, and I, along with our two young boys, were thrust into the most difficult chapter of our lives. Without warning, Josh was diagnosed with Stage Four high-grade small-cell neuroendocrine carcinoma—an extremely rare cancer that carries an almost-inescapable death sentence. Ten months later, Josh died, and at the age of 39, I was plunged simultaneously into widowhood and single-motherhood.

Throughout my family's ordeal and its aftermath, I kept a journal, chronicling the many stages of my journey with Josh, both throughout his illness and after his death. One day, while still deep in my grief, I sat down to re-read my entries, hoping to find some solace and understanding in what I had written. At every turn, I discovered what I had known all along—that my faith and trust in God's plan—as well as the faith that Josh found before he died—had carried us through the hardest of life's challenges. And, since that time, His light has continued to illuminate my path, giving my life new meaning and a sense of joy I never thought possible.

I have written this account of my journey to give others hope as they process loss, in all its various forms, and to help survivors find positive ways to move forward and recapture the beauty they have lost in their own lives.

Dr. Angela Lindenmuth Marick
York, Pennsylvania
May 2018

CHAPTER 1

Life Unravels

Wednesday, July 1, 2015

"Ange, I need you to take me to the hospital."

I was trying to calm my anxiousness as I heard my husband, Josh, get out of bed and pace the room for what felt like the hundredth time. It was 5 a.m.

You know how some men seriously regress when they get sick? The ones that need you to do everything for them because they feel like they are *dying* on the couch—and they just have a sore throat? That wasn't Josh. His arm could be falling off, and he wouldn't complain. So, when he asked me to take him to the hospital, I jumped into action.

I rushed him to the emergency room, less than 10 minutes away, so full of anxiety, and dropped him off at the front door. We had two young, sleeping children at home—Justin (10) and Carter (7)—and I needed to get back to them. As a mom and wife, I was torn. I didn't want to leave my husband without having a clue as to what was causing his symptoms, but my children needed one of us to be there when they woke up. It didn't even cross my mind to call a friend to go over to the house and cover for me. Asking for help was a completely foreign concept at that moment. It was taking all of my brainpower to focus on the immediacy of the now.

Later that morning, I took the boys to park camp as usual.

I wanted to keep their routine as normal as possible so they wouldn't catch on to the potentially serious situation unraveling at the hospital near our home in York, Pennsylvania. I woodenly told the counselors that we had a family emergency and wasn't sure what was going on but to keep a close eye on our boys. My mind was trying unsuccessfully to make sense of why my strong husband, who had always been a Superman, was suddenly lying in a hospital bed.

When I returned to Josh's side, I found a team of interns in his room. As I soon discovered, July 1 was the day they started their residency training. As you can imagine, few of them knew what they were supposed to do. Even Josh joked that he had to help them operate some of the machinery. It didn't give me much confidence in the medical staff.

The doctors were scratching their heads, not knowing what was wrong with my husband. His temperature had spiked to 102°, and his face was flushed with fever. At one point, one of the newly-appointed residents told us Josh might need to be quarantined for infectious disease, as he clearly had an infection, even though they didn't know what was causing it. Josh said he'd felt a swelling in his upper abdomen since the day before, and it had gotten progressively worse. They whisked him away to CT, where a scan revealed a mass in his abdominal region.

Differential diagnoses were considered. Was it an abscess? Was it lymphoma? Was it a life-threatening infection? The more he was tested, the more questions remained unanswered.

Two days before our nightmare began, Josh had treated our lawn to get rid of the infestation of weeds in our overgrown backyard. He went to bed as usual but kept waking up to pee. He thought perhaps it was because he'd inhaled the lawn chemicals. Astoundingly, when he weighed himself the next morning, he had dropped, overnight, from 199 to 188 pounds.

That whole next day, he felt sluggish and nauseous. He even came home from work early and sent me to the store to buy anti-nausea remedies. None of them relieved his discomfort. Then came the night he spent pacing back and forth, wondering what was causing him such distress. Later we would learn that all the while, a small lump had started growing in his upper belly.

I remember standing in the claustrophobic hospital room, staring at my husband and the surreal surroundings. How could this be happening? It can't be anything serious. Nothing terribly serious happens to us. We've been fortunate to coast through life with minimal speed bumps. But, what if it *is* something serious? For the first time, I wondered, "Will our lives be changed by this?" So many questions flooded my brain as I hazily observed the man I had married 14 years earlier.

Josh had always been healthy. He had run a marathon in D.C. just that previous October. He was a running machine. He reminded me of Forrest Gump—he would just keep running. No physical exertion, however extreme, seemed to strain him or break him. He was rarely sick, except for a five-year period of time, starting around my pregnancy with Justin, when he had experienced a bout of ulcerative colitis. And lately, come to think of it, he hadn't been eating or sleeping very well, either.

After a while, Josh insisted that I go to back to work. Reluctantly, I left the hospital and drove to my office to go through the motions of my morning routine as a wellness chiropractor.

The day ended with no further understanding of what was triggering the growing mass in my husband's belly. No answers, just continued uncertainty. The doctors had started Josh on IV antibiotics, and his fever had abated a little. I went to bed that night, alone, telling myself all would be well and we'd find the answers and solutions we sought very soon.

Josh had been in the hospital for three days when the doctors finally decided to aspirate the mass. It was making him nauseous and weaker by the day and had grown to a point where it had made it difficult for Josh to eat. They pulled out many cc's of fluid, which gave him some relief. At last, he was able to take in a meal.

The results of the test showed the presence of a particular kind of bacteria that is only supposed to live in your intestines. This confirmed that he was septic. Sepsis is a very serious condition. It can occur when your intestines have a hole through

3

which contents can spill out into the abdominal cavity. From there, bacteria can spread all over, causing massive reactions in the body. If untreated (and sometimes even when treated), a person can die within a few days.

When Josh wasn't napping or trying to do some work on his laptop, he was researching everything he could to figure out what was going on in his body. He was not the kind to just let things happen. He wanted to know every detail of each possible cause and its outcome. Meanwhile, the doctors remained puzzled.

Saturday, July 4

When the Fourth of July came around, Josh was still in the hospital. His room had a lovely view, overlooking the local baseball stadium where that evening they'd be shooting off the fiery rockets we all looked forward to every year. That night, our two boys curled up on Josh's bed and excitedly watched the magnificent fireworks display. It was beautiful, but it didn't keep my unsettled mind off the plethora of unknowns we were facing. At least, I thought, we were together as a family....

Thursday, July 9

A full week after Josh entered the hospital, the pressure and discomfort in his abdomen was worse than ever. The doctors sent him back to interventional radiology (IR) to see if they could aspirate the mass again. They quickly determined that there was far less fluid than before and that the mass was indeed solid. The IR took a needle biopsy, then told us that there was nothing more they could do. We were unceremoniously released from the hospital to await the results of his test. Meantime, because some fluid remained, Josh had a drain placed his abdomen. Now he would have to navigate a long tube sticking out of his belly with a bulb at the end that needed regular changing.

Once we got home, I encouraged Josh to go for a walk with me. My marathon-running husband had the plodding gait and speed of a 90-year-old, but he kept that sweet smile on his face as he slowly pushed his six-foot-one frame around the block in our neighborhood. Our boys were so happy to have Daddy home, though they weren't aware of how sick their Superman Daddy really was.

Over the weekend, Josh's mass continued to grow, as did our anxiety as to what could possibly be the cause.

Monday, July 13

Thankfully, when Monday morning arrived, Josh received the long-awaited phone call from one of his doctors at the hospital. He told Josh that he should come in that morning to go over his test results. As one would imagine, Josh asked, "Is it serious?" The doctor replied, "It's fine," still, he should come in to discuss his condition. I remember Josh saying that if the results turned out to be serious, he was going to be upset that the doctor had implied all would be well. With the expectation of good results, Josh insisted that I go to work. I, in turn, insisted that he take his Dad with him to his appointment.

Josh was an incredible man for many reasons, and I admired him in so many ways. His ability to be independent was wonderful most of the time. However, as a natural nurturer, it was hard for me not to be involved in every step of his care. But he would insist that I act normally and go to work.

That morning, I was very distracted. In between patients, I kept running back to my office to check my phone for updates. My heart raced every time I pushed the button to see if any messages had come through. Mid-morning, I pushed the button, and a message popped up. It read: "It's a neuroendocrine tumor." He said tumor—not cancer, but even though I'm not an oncologist or well-versed on different types of cancer, I knew this wasn't good. My mind started racing. *What does this mean? What do we do? What are the treatment options? Is it progressive? I must be dreaming. This can't be possible! And why in hell am I still at the office working, while he's alone processing this crazy diagnosis?*

Tears raced down my cheeks as the word "tumor" sank into my completely frozen brain. I felt my heart starting to break. I tried to build a wall around it so I could keep my shit together and do what I had to do—take care of my patients for a little while longer until I could be by my husband's side and figure this out. I cried silently for a few minutes to release some of the grief so I could return to my duties.

I'll never forget the first patient I saw right after I got the news. In my shock and disbelief, I tried to go through the motions of caring for her, but I felt hollow and couldn't focus. I'm usually a sunny and optimistic person, so she knew right away that something was wrong. She stood there with genuine concern and looked right into my heart—and she saw it. She saw my raw shock and confusion and asked, what was the trouble? Her compassion undid me. I told her my news about the diagnosis and my fear of what it was going to do to my husband, our family, our present, and our future. The hug she gave me infused me with the strength I needed to fulfill my responsibilities that morning.

At lunchtime, my Mom and I joined Josh at Panera so he could download the details of his newly determined diagnosis. He looked at me intently and asked, "What questions do you have?" Of course, I had a million—but first I needed to know: Is this cancer? He then revealed the dreaded news: "Yes, it is cancer." The official name was "high-grade small-cell neuroendocrine carcinoma."

Neither of us had expected cancer. I mean, who does? That doesn't happen to us. That happens to other nameless, faceless people. My shell-shocked mind wasn't equipped to handle this information. I couldn't fathom what this diagnosis really meant. I have always focused on the positive aspects of life, no matter the situation. But not this time. This was incomprehensible. It went in the opposite direction of all that I had ever known. I didn't know how to process such negative thoughts. I'd never had to confront them before. Both of our families had experienced cancer, but it had affected our grandparents when they were much, much older than we were.

My mind clamped down like a sphincter, and it refused to consider any of the worst possible outcomes. I shifted into survival mode and pushed all negativity far, far away and focused on the man in front of me.

I observed Josh as we ate our salads. He was calm and very matter-of-fact as he answered all of our questions. Finally, I asked, "What do we do now?" He said the local doctor wanted him to see an oncologist and get a PET scan within the next two weeks. Then, unbelievably, he suggested that I go back to work while he returned home to research his illness.

From the moment he heard the diagnosis, Josh had been researching like crazy. He quickly discovered that not only was it cancer, but it was also an extremely rare and aggressive form of it. That meant research on it was probably minimal, and successful treatment options would be limited. Unsettled by the doctor's apparent lack of urgency, Josh started looking for a doctor in our greater metropolitan area with firsthand experience with this type of cancer.

We decided to share the news with our sons that night during a family walk around the block. When Josh told them that he had cancer and explained what that meant, they both excitedly asked if he would lose his hair. Josh, who had beautiful head of thick, dark hair, said, yes, that might happen. They thought he should get a big frizzy wig, and that it would look awesome on him. Josh laughed and told the boys that they had been the most fun to tell his news to that day. He and I looked at each other in relief as our boys took the news and chose to see it from a funny perspective.

Our kids were never anxious kids. Highly intelligent, they both knew what cancer meant, but they had been blessed with healthy doses of optimism. They could only imagine a positive outcome for the Dad they saw as indestructible.

Josh quickly found an experienced oncologist in Baltimore, Dr. Sandy Kotiah, a brilliant, no-nonsense, and deeply caring doctor, who was familiar with Josh's cancer. When she saw his pathology report, she insisted he come to her office the very next day.

Wednesday, July 15

Again, Josh's Dad went with him to his appointment. I stayed back to keep my business open, while the boys happily went to day camp. I was grateful for that. They knew Dad was sick, but, as we didn't have any answers, we were reluctant to tell them too much.

That afternoon, Josh phoned to say his new oncologist was adamant that he be admitted to Baltimore's Mercy Hospital right away. She wanted him to start chemotherapy immediately. The first line of attack was a regimen of Cisplatin and Etoposide, platinum-based chemotherapy drugs that were developed in the 80s. The treatment plan consisted of three days of chemo and then three weeks off, for six rounds.

After work, I raced down I-83 to be by his side. There he was, in his hospital bed, laughing with the nurses and calmly waiting for his first round of chemo to begin. He was relieved to know that his aggressive cancer was finally being addressed by an oncologist who recognized that his diagnosis required immediate attention.

That same night, Josh had another CT scan. His tumor had grown to 10 cm, and Dr. Kotiah said there was evidence it had spread to his liver. Within two weeks of Josh feeling the bulge in his belly, it had spread to his liver. She looked at him gravely and asked, "You know what that means, right?" Josh answered in the affirmative, but I refused to accept the implicit prognosis. The cancer had spread to another organ, which meant Josh was already at Stage Four, with a life-expectancy of about four months. *What????!!!!*

I left the hospital that night in complete meltdown mode. Suddenly, my world had become unfamiliar and surreal. The flood of tears made it difficult to navigate my SUV out of the parking garage. I pulled over and called my friend Troy. He was in the middle of a business dinner but instantly excused himself to listen to my heart-breaking news. I finally gave in to the overwhelming emotions I'd kept barricaded for the past two weeks and started sobbing.

Troy had been my business coach since 2009 and was my

friend, mentor, colleague, and confidant. He had helped me through the ups and downs of trying to build a business while simultaneously raising a family. I didn't know how to articulate what I was feeling or how to process the information. But he gave me the space I needed to break down and release my heavy burden. He didn't try to mollify me, he just listened patiently. As I calmed down, he offered up the words that I needed to hear: He said he believed I had the strength and ability to weather this new chapter in my life. His positive encouragement gave me the fortitude to get home. On the drive back, I started reminiscing about all the things Josh and I had done together, the life we had built together, and how much we'd always meant to each other.

CHAPTER 2

Beginnings

"Ange, let's go down to Lenroc and hang out with the guys down there," my friend Jen suggested. It was the day before Thanksgiving break, and I was in my first semester, majoring in pre-med, at Cornell University in Ithaca, New York.

"Sure," I replied, mildly apprehensive about going to a fraternity to meet new guys. I wasn't sure if I would fit in the scene there but hoped I'd be accepted and meet someone nice. The fashionista in me that November of 1995 chose to wear a baggy flannel shirt and overalls, with my hair pulled up into a high ponytail.

As my two friends, Jen and Michelle, started a conversation with two of the frat boys, I was drawn to another. His name was Joshua Andrew Lindenmuth. We sat and talked, and among many things, he told me about his many travels around the world with his family. I had only been to Canada and was fascinated by his stories. He asked me a lot of questions about my life. I was both impressed and pleased that he appeared to be interested in me, as a person. I flashed my blinding smile at him many times that evening. The metal braces on my teeth must have hypnotized him into continuing our conversation.

Josh was the first man I'd met in college who seemed genuinely interested in knowing who I was. He was eager to engage in conversations beyond the weather or what classes we were taking. We spent that night talking on a couch until 6 a.m. I was 19. He was 20. Within a few weeks, we made our couplehood official and stepped out in fancy dress at his fraternity's winter formal. A month later, we shyly confessed our love for each other and embarked on a deeply loving courtship.

I need to add one caveat here. Josh was a wonderful boyfriend to me. He was also the most honest person I knew. Normally, that would be a wonderful trait. But a year into our relationship, he told me he thought he should be dating other women while he was in college. He had never had a serious girlfriend before and thought it wise to explore other relationships. How else was he to know that I was really the one for him, for the rest of our lives? As you can imagine, I was less than thrilled about this, but I loved and respected him enough to endure a separation. So, In the spirit of true transparency, we broke up a couple of times and sought out new relationships. They all fizzled quickly. It didn't take us long to recognize that we only wanted each other.

Josh had tried several different majors while in college. When we met, he was transitioning into Cornell's world-renowned School of Hotel Administration, having already tried his hand at physics and pre-med. He had quickly discovered that his brain wasn't suited for hotel management and opted instead to apply to Cornell's very competitive and rigorous engineering program. The first time he applied, his application was thrown out. No one had ever gone from hotel management into engineering, and the admissions department thought it was a joke. Josh responded that he was fully committed to doing the work, so they reluctantly admitted him into the program. By this time, he had only two years left before graduating, and he was determined to finish on time. His parents had already been kind enough to help him out financially with school, so he refused their generous offer to pay for an additional year. Nor did he want to go into debt just because he'd changed majors.

Josh soon discovered that his mind worked like an engineer's. For once, he wasn't having to memorize terms but was applying his very robust left brain to problem-solving. Even though he was saddled with 26 credit hours a semester (while also working as

11

a teaching assistant in the computer lab), his GPA, unbelievably, went up. He had finally found the school he was destined for. After many all-nighters and sober weekends, Josh not only graduated on time but with the distinction of cum laude for his 3.65 GPA.

Josh was interested in so many things—from string theory to partial differential equations—that he decided the world of consulting would be a good fit for him. Consulting projects were ever-revolving and would give him a chance to work with smart, forward-thinking young people. He took a job with Accenture, formerly Andersen Consulting, and moved to Chicago. I still had one more year at Cornell to finish my pre-med degree. I would take the Amtrak train from Syracuse to Chicago as often as I could to visit him. I hated the long distance between us, but we managed to survive the year apart.

By the time I graduated, I was convinced that a medical doctor's life wasn't right for me. At this point, I just wanted to be with my man, so I decided to move out to Chicago and take the easiest job I could get. For my first grown-up job in the real world, I settled for a management training program at Sears. It was horrible. I quickly learned that settling for something you don't like can be as miserable as it is unfulfilling. Then, a few months after moving to Chi-Town, I became acquainted with a chiropractor. I had a preconceived notion that chiropractors were nothing more than wannabe medical doctors with no real expertise. But, as I got to know this intelligent man and saw how his patients were getting better without drugs or surgery, I realized that this was a career that would suit me. When I called Josh to tell him I wanted to be a chiropractor, he was supremely skeptical. But, when he realized how much it meant to me to be able to help others in the arenas of health and well-being, he began to support my decision.

In March 2000, Josh helped me move to Davenport, Iowa, where I began my training at Palmer College of Chiropractic. It was the first thing in my life that I had done completely on my own. No one was telling me to do this. I wasn't following anyone. I, alone, had made the decision. At the age of 23, I began to feel empowered as an individual. Meanwhile, Josh remained in Chicago.

Over that summer, Josh and I began to look at engagement rings. He would tease me and say he wasn't going to ask me for a while yet. It would drive me crazy. We both knew we were going to end up together, so why wait? Finally, on Sunday, September 10, 2000, while sitting at a table in the back of the Celebration Belle—a fully functional paddleboat that meandered down the Mississippi River—Josh got down on one knee, presented me with a ring, and asked me to be his wife. I think I said yes. Seriously, I ecstatically replied, "Yes!" and nearly knocked him over with a bear hug.

It had been quite a process for Josh to pick out my engagement ring. He was reluctant to part with a lot of money for a piece of jewelry. He preferred to spend money on experiences. Nevertheless, he knew it was important to me, so he had looked high and low to find the perfect one at just the right price. He had traveled to Chicago, Toronto, New York City, and even his hometown of York to find the best match. He eventually settled on a diamond that he found on Blue Nile and a setting he discovered in the jewelry district of Chicago. It was a beautiful platinum ring with four small 0.1 carat clear diamond baguettes and a 0.6 carat high-quality, round-cut diamond in the center. I loved that ring! Not only because of the quality of it but the fact that my man had spent so much time to find something perfect because he cared about my happiness.

CHAPTER 3

Marriage and Family

Josh and I were married on June 23, 2001, at my family's church in Rochester, New York. We invited 165 guests and had six bridesmaids and just as many groomsmen. The day turned out to be 60 degrees and overcast with some rain. I chose to think the rain was God blessing us. I remember walking down the aisle on the arm of my Dad as he jokingly told me how much money each of those steps was costing him. It was a good thing I was the only daughter! As we slowly made our way towards the alter, I remembered to take deep breaths. As I did so, I swear I felt God's hand on my shoulder, assuring me this was part of His plan. Josh was meant to be my husband, and I his wife. I felt at peace, and with joyful tears I committed my life to the man I had been with for five years. We were then 24 and 25 years old. We had no idea where life would take us or what highs and lows life would throw our way. But we put such thoughts on hold and enjoyed a blissful twelve-day honeymoon in Aruba.

Then it was back to chiropractic school. At that time, Josh was traveling to such places as Michigan and Wisconsin to work on whatever project Accenture had assigned to him. While he was away during the week, I threw all of my energy into school, buckled down, and studied hard. I was committed to learning all that I could with the intention of helping my future patients as best as I could. On June 20, 2003, I was honored to graduate as class valedictorian.

Immediately following the ceremony, Josh took me on my first trip to Europe to celebrate. We toured Paris, Florence, Vienna, and Munich. We walked miles upon miles every day, exploring the unique beauty of each city and getting to know the different peoples. I'd never been overseas before and was experiencing a whole new level of culture.

Then came the time for us to decide where to settle down. We decided to rent an apartment in York, Pennsylvania, where a job opportunity had turned up for me. Josh had grown up in York and had no desire to return to his hometown. But because he was traveling and loved what he was doing, he agreed to the move.

Josh and I settled into a routine. He would fly out of Baltimore-Washington Airport early Monday morning and return Thursday night. I worked Monday through Friday and most Saturdays. Some Monday mornings, I would cry when Josh left. I didn't want to make him feel bad, but I couldn't help myself. I missed him during the week. I'd get lonely going to bed every night without him. I had already been doing that for two years, but then I'd been in school, surrounded by friends.

At school, I had aced so many tests and projects, I thought I knew everything I needed to know to enter the non-academic world. But when I started my new position as an associate doctor at a large chiropractic office, I quickly understood that no amount of book smarts compares with the knowledge gained from working with real patients.

Over time, I started mentioning the "B" word with Josh. I wanted to start a family sooner rather than later. We had been together many years, and I was ready to have a baby. We were in a financially secure situation at this point, so I also thought it was time to buy a house. We looked for a year. Josh had very specific criteria for where we should or shouldn't live. He didn't want to live in a cookie-cutter neighborhood, where all the homes were the same; he wanted to pay a very fair price; and he wanted to be close to the highway.

Throughout this time, while we were looking at homes and contemplating having babies, I was starting to make it clear that I wanted my husband to be home during the week. It was time for him to find a job that would allow him to be home every night so that we could raise our family together. He quickly realized that suitable jobs for him were scarce in York. He'd have to look farther afield. At last he settled for one in Towson, Maryland, just north of Baltimore, where he'd be managing the technology department for a small payroll company. The only drawback was that he'd have an 80-mile roundtrip commute.

By May 2004, after just one month of trying to conceive, I discovered that all our parts worked and I was expecting. We still were looking for the perfect home. Josh, concerned about the expenses a baby can bring, felt more compelled than ever to stay in an apartment rather than buy a house. Now that he had such a long commute, he was less than thrilled with the thought of adding on the responsibilities of homeownership.

Josh was like that, always looking down the road and taking steps to prepare. Before we bought our first home, he designed a computer program to determine what our monthly utility bill would be based on the square footage of the house with the thermostat set at various temperatures. The overly cautious attention he paid to such details made me laugh. But his commitment to our family's financial security was a wonderful gift that I would certainly grow to appreciate in the years to come.

In June, I found my dream house. It was located in a pretty, well-established neighborhood with good schools and a beautiful park nearby. It was also close to the highway to Baltimore. Before committing to the purchase, I had an ultrasound. Josh wanted to make sure that there was only one baby in my uterus. His thinking was that, if there were two babies on the way, financially we shouldn't move forward on a house. But, in my mind, that would be all the more reason to have *more* space. When the ultrasound showed only one fetus, we signed the contract and purchased our home in August 2004.

Two months later, at 26 weeks pregnant, I found myself on

bed rest with an irritable uterus. This meant I had been overdoing things and had started going into pre-term labor. At the time, I'd been teaching strength training and step classes at a local gym as well as working six days a week as a chiropractor. I was naïve. I had felt great, so I never thought of changing my level of activity—until the contractions came on and wouldn't relent.

As I lay in the hospital for a week trying to get my cranky uterus to calm down, Josh was busy researching all there was to know about my situation and what could be done. We didn't like the idea of pumping all kinds of meds into my body. Josh found an article on a study that had been conducted on sheep that suggested that taking high doses of an omega-3 supplement would slow down contractions. Between the IV magnesium (a natural muscle relaxant) I was given in the hospital and the omega-3 supplements I was taking at home, I was released from bed rest after four weeks. I went back to work and happily enjoyed the rest of the pregnancy.

On January 14, 2005, at 8:40 a.m. after laboring throughout night, Justin Connor joined our family. The first thing I remember was feeling slightly panicked and thinking, "Holy crap, we are responsible for this helpless little thing!" But the fear quickly passed, and I felt nothing but gratitude as Josh and I immediately started to bond with our beautiful, precious baby boy.

January was always a particularly crazy time for Josh at the payroll company. Everyone would be busy working overtime, getting W-2's ready for their clients. On the Friday Justin was born, Josh received many phone calls from his colleagues. But, they weren't calling to offer congratulations—they were calling to ask him to fix the various problems that had come up in his absence. I couldn't believe it! I assumed everyone got a reprieve from work on the day of their child's birth. I had much to learn about life. Josh returned to the office the following Monday to put out all of the miscellaneous fires. Thankfully, my Mom came up and stayed with us for two weeks as I figured out the new baby thing as well as the nursing thing.

I remember feeling overwhelmed when Justin was born. I

started grieving for the time Josh and I would no longer have to ourselves. Date nights would be less frequent. Alone time would require planning. And just as we were adjusting to our new family paradigm of three, Josh told me that he didn't like living in York. His long commute made him feel disconnected from me and the baby, not to mention it had put a real damper on our social life. He'd had dreams of running his own company one day and felt trapped in the daily grind of juggling work and a domestic life. Plus, he had only relented in buying the house because he knew it would make me happy. But he clearly wasn't.

Even though Josh was less than thrilled with some aspects of his life, he remained committed to working down in Towson. His team was growing, and he threw enormous energy into helping the business grow. Sometimes he put in 80-hour weeks. He would come home late most nights, except Mondays when he would pick Justin up from daycare at 6 p.m. He loved being a father and engaged Justin in all kinds of play as he became more interactive. Josh even wrote down all the words Justin knew at 16 months (he knew 60). Justin loved being the center of attention and always wanted to be with us.

In the summer of 2006, when Justin was about 18 months old, I brought up the subject of having another baby. Josh wasn't so keen on it. He hadn't been feeling too well around this time. He was stressed out and couldn't fully wrap his mind around having the responsibility of another child, at least not while he was so consumed with work and experiencing chronic bouts of colitis. But I, being ever persistent, had made up my mind. He gave in to my dreams, and we started trying.

Much to my disappointment, I didn't become pregnant right away. I would sit in church, by myself, and pray. I prayed to God, saying that I recognized He was truly in control and that I believed in him. Miraculously, a few weeks later, my prayers were answered.

On December 31, 2006, after five months of trying, I discovered I was pregnant. I joyfully woke my sleeping husband to show him the stick with two clear lines on it. When I told Josh that God had heard my prayer, he humored me with a smile, but I could tell he was dismissive of my trust and faith in God's divine intervention.

A few months later, I started to experience some bleeding that gradually grew in intensity. I was diagnosed with a subchorionic hemorrhage—essentially a tear between the placenta and uterus. Subsequently, I was put on bed rest and remained in that status for 20 weeks. I remember in my 14th week of pregnancy, I prayed to God to either take this baby if he or she was not going to make it to term or to give me a sign that all would be okay. Almost immediately, I felt the hint of a kick. It could have been gas, but I chose to believe it was my little developing baby letting me know that all would be okay.

It was a *long* 20 weeks of sitting. But I kept busy, enjoying visits from family and friends as well as blogging, reading, and watching movies. I would constantly visualize having a healthy, natural delivery. I figured if I had to be inactive for five months, I should at least have a healthy delivery. Sure enough, on August 16, at 10:45 p.m., I felt a pop and a gush of fluid. At first I worried that it might be more blood but was quickly relieved to see it was clear fluid. Contractions started soon after.

Just as I called out to him to get ready to go to the hospital, Josh, who had a sixth sense about my impending labor, was just hitting the send button to his workplace to let them know he would not be in the next day.

I labored on a therapy ball most of the night. I was so relieved that my body was doing what it had been designed to do after spending so many months sitting on the couch. Six hours after going into labor, I gratefully delivered a healthy and absolutely adorable little boy, Carter Jackson Lindenmuth. I must be honest though, labor hurt like hell, and apparently I was swearing and screaming that I would die. I don't remember the latter part, but that was what Josh told me. When Carter finally entered the world, I looked over at my life partner and saw that he had been crying, and his shirt was wet with tears. I think seeing me in such excruciating pain had almost been too much for him. Together we wept in gratitude for the healthy birth of our youngest son.

CHAPTER 4

Life Happens

I had started going to church with Justin, but Josh hardly ever came. He would ask me if I'd rather he work Sunday morning and have family time later, or come to church and work the rest of the day. I always looked forward to family time, so I would agree to the former.

That was the trouble. He was always working. Josh had this laser-like ability to focus on his work, and he'd expound at length about whatever project he was tackling. I'd seen the same pattern when he worked at Accenture. He would often work 100-hour weeks, becoming completely engaged—not just to finish the project but also to find ways to help the client make the company more efficient. And now at his job in Towson, he wanted to see the business grow and would move mountains to make it happen.

Josh would often come home from work well after 8 p.m., then hang out with the family for a short while. He rarely watched TV. He scoffed at it, saying it interfered with people connecting with one another. But then he'd go back into the office that adjoined the kitchen of our house. The room was a conglomeration of organized chaos. He was brilliant, and yet he would sit surrounded by piles of random notes scribbled in his unique messy printing. His staff would routinely get emails sent at 2 a.m. Over time, I accepted this way of life because if Josh wasn't getting something done, he'd be even more stressed.

But at the heart of everything, Josh always let us know how important we all were to him. He made sure that I knew he adored me and made me feel I was the most beautiful and loving woman. He also made sure to take time with each of the boys. When they were little, he'd make their stuffed animals "talk" to them. And he was marvelous at speaking to them like they were young men rather than small children. As the boys grew older, Josh engaged them in more cerebral activities. For instance, he once helped them program robotic Legos that could shoot darts across the room.

Josh had no interest in material things. He preferred to spend his money and energy on experiences with his family. In 2012, he convinced me to go to Greece with him to run a marathon. According to legend, in 490 B.C. a Greek messenger named Philippides ran from the battlefield at Marathon to Athens to report the Greeks' victory over the Persians. (The story also says that he then collapsed and died.) We flew 5,000 miles to run the legendary route. This was the first trip we had taken without the children for any length of time.

The race started in Marathon and ended in Athens, a distance of 26.2 miles. Josh ran with such ease that it didn't even faze him. I, on the other hand, being a mere mortal, was wary of the challenge but managed to go the distance without completely destroying myself in the process.

We decided to recover with a week's rest on Santorini, an incredible, whitewashed Greek island paradise that boasted ancient ruins and three colors of sand—black, red, and white. Josh always showed me affection and never wavered in his love for me. But, because we were both always busy with work, we hadn't really connected in quite some time. Now, for the first time in a long time, I didn't have to compete for attention with his work or my own endless cycle of cleaning the house, wiping poopy butts and runny noses—and building up a business. As the stress fell away, we fully engaged with one another. We hadn't had that in years. I remember thinking, "Oh…I remember you. You're the guy I met at the alter all those years ago." Josh, on the other hand, would always claim that we'd never had to work at our marriage and had stayed in the honeymoon phase ever since the wedding.

We returned home in our newfound marital bliss. We committed to spending more one-on-one time together and made more room for private conversations and other intimacies. As our relationship grew into a new level of maturity, Josh said he needed more balance in his life and more of a social life. For a long time, he'd spent his days alone in his office with no one to talk to, communicating mostly by way of his computer. He would come home feeling almost depressed and cut off from the world. He was desperate for a social outlet.

The year before, Josh had hired a woman named Karen, and they'd hit it off immediately. She was smart and a hard worker and Josh enjoyed the friendship they had formed. He soon met her boyfriend, Scott, and her sister, Sarah, all of whom worked in Baltimore. Karen, Sarah, and Josh would regularly meet up after work, go running, and train for races together. Josh was so happy to have real companions he could to talk to. Sometimes, he'd stay to have dinner with them, their father, Mel, and their stepmother, Trish, a nurse at Mercy Hospital (and to whom I will always be grateful for smoothing our way on so many hospital visits).

After Josh started running with his friends, I could tell that, bit by bit, his chronic stress was lifting. I was never jealous of the time the three shared together. I knew their friendship was special and filled a void that Josh had felt for many years. I was happy to see him come home at night more energized.

Their friendship was beneficial to me in another way. I am an early riser. Josh was not. Before he met Karen and Sarah, he would come home from work and want to be Chatty Cathy, whereas once the kids went down at 8:30, I would be ready for the soothing comfort of our bed. He no longer came home needing to chat now that he had new outlets for non-work related conversations.

Karen and Sarah welcomed me into their lives wholeheartedly. I was so grateful to them for providing the friendship Josh so desperately needed. I couldn't see them often, as I would be busy with the office or running the kids here and there. But when we got together, we always enjoyed each other's company.

As the days flew by, Josh and I continued squeezing in date nights, juggling work, and trying to balance our lives as much as possible. I took on the lion's share of household duties. I had become the Director of Logistics in our house. I would coordinate the kids' schedules with babysitters and activities, as Josh wasn't usually home when the kids went to bed, and in the morning he'd wake up after they'd already left for school. I also took up most of the yardwork. I figured since he was working so many hours to provide for us, I could do everything else. It was our unspoken division of labor. I worked at the office just three days a week, which gave me the flexibility to do chores on the off days. We made it happen. I let go of wanting him to take on more of the domestic responsibilities because it didn't seem possible with our current arrangement. I figured out how to make peace with it. I also made sure to take time to care for myself, so I could give my best to not only to my family but to my beloved staff and patients as well. On my days off, I took the time to exercise regularly; treat myself to monthly facials and an occasional massage; schedule lunches with precious friends and colleagues; and research ways to help build my practice. Looking back now on all that got done, I am so grateful I was able to maintain my sanity and positive disposition. It was a lot!

For someone who doesn't like to be alone, I sure felt like I did a lot alone. I went to many school and social functions sans Josh, as he would be working. It did eat at me at times, but I knew it wasn't in my power to change it.

When Josh was deeply discouraged about his life—feeling trapped in a job he wasn't always enthusiastic about, tired of his long commute, or disengaged socially—he would confide in me that sometimes he'd daydream about being hit by a bus. He explained that he didn't want to die—he just wanted to be hurt badly enough that he'd be forced to do something different with his life. I hated hearing that. It made me feel so utterly helpless as well as guilty for my part in having set the course of our lives.

He wasn't living the life he had dreamed of. Josh had always been drawn to cities. In his twenties, he had imagined living in New York City and working on Wall Street. But, as two different people who had come together in marriage, we recognized that we had to find ways to adapt, compromise, and blend our dreams and expectations in order to move forward successfully, both as a family and as a happily married couple.

Josh and I had spent our whole adult life together. Sometimes, I felt we were fully connected. But, there were other times I felt we were living separate lives, side-by-side but with very different responsibilities and experiences. In truth, sometimes I longed for him to take a more active role in our day-to-day home life and not have to feel that it was all on me. I wouldn't have minded if he'd asked how he could help me out, especially on some of the really tough days.

On February 1, 2015, after I'd returned from a chiropractic seminar in Las Vegas, Josh woke me up in the middle of the night. He had been working downstairs, and I had fallen asleep, exhausted from the long flight. "Ange," he said, "if I'm gone someday, I know you will be okay."

"What? What are you talking about?" My sleepy mind was not grasping what he was saying.

"Ange, seriously. If I'm not here someday, you will be okay," he insisted.

"Josh, is something wrong?"

"Not right now. I just want you to know that." And that was all I could get out of him. I went back to sleep, but, of course, the conversation stuck in my head. I chalked it up with a few other bizarre things he had said to me. More than once throughout our marriage, he had mentioned that he did not expect to live a long life.

Five months passed without further incident. And then, just like that, our reasonably predictable, secure life vanished....

CHAPTER 5

The New Normal

Saturday, July 18

After three days in the hospital, Josh was released with a freshly installed PowerPort infused with harsh chemicals to annihilate the cancer that had been growing in his body. Much to our surprise, he felt great and was starting to feel relief from the pressure in his belly that had been causing him such discomfort for half a month. We were both thankful that, for the time being, the chemo seemed to be doing its job. The only silver lining to aggressively growing cancer is that it can respond very quickly to chemotherapy treatment. Thankfully, Josh's cancer responded.

During this time, the owners of Josh's company scheduled a trip to Florida. When the car service arrived, the driver that morning was a woman named Gloria, an immigrant from South Africa and the owner of the company. Gloria told them that, inexplicably, she had felt compelled to drive that day instead of assigning the job to one of her employees, as she normally would have. She sensed there was a problem with her passengers and asked if something was troubling them. They admitted they had just heard that Josh, one of their employees, had received very grim news about his health. As a committed Christian woman, Gloria asked them if Josh believed in God. When they said they weren't sure, she pressed them. Would he be willing to talk to her?

Again, they didn't know the answer but promised to pass her offer along when they returned home.

Josh did not have a strong faith. He believed in a higher power but had never been a particularly spiritual person. He often chose to work Sunday mornings when I went to church with the boys. I've always felt that one's spiritual journey is very personal, so while I always encouraged him to join me, I knew not to push. He needed to find his own path. On the other hand, Josh was always willing to talk to anyone about anything. So he agreed to let Gloria get in touch with him.

Always the skeptic and seeker of tangible proof, he was initially turned off by her persistent encouragement to turn to Him. But she would push Josh to put his trust in God. After a while, he agreed to begin praying daily, even though at first he felt very awkward.

Josh returned to work at his company one week after leaving the hospital. His mind was never quiet, and he had an insatiable need to be doing something productive at all times. He also wanted to start running again. We didn't know if running would trigger any side effects, so I insisted that he always have someone run with him. Our friend Sarah happily agreed to accompany him. As soon as Josh started running again, he began to feel stronger.

Who does that? I mean, he started this crazy intense chemo and then jumped right into rigorous exercise. He told me, "Ange, I want to make sure that I do everything I can to be healthy and get through this. If I don't make it through, I want to know that I did everything I could." He was emphatic about this.

When Josh wasn't working, he immersed himself in researching his diagnosis and all the different non-traditional methods he could try to help his body fight off the cancer. He eliminated sugar from his diet because it's linked to inflammation, and also because cancer loves to feast on sugar. He started taking a series of different supplements to support his body and reduce inflammation. We had so many bottles of supplements lying around the kitchen that it was hard to find counter space to cook. At one point, he wanted to try an antibiotic that is given to farm animals because he read that it could have a positive impact on cancer. Unfortunately, due to strict regulations, he wasn't able to acquire it. It was probably just as well because it required a precise amount to be helpful, and anything beyond that amount could have been harmful.

As Josh experimented with his diet, I tried to figure out how to manage everyone's food preferences. He would read various studies to inform his nutritional choices, and every article brought a new recommendation. It drove me crazy from day-to-day, trying to figure out what he would or would not eat. At one point, he subsisted on smoothies made with olive oil and chocolate-flavored protein. He drank a whole bottle of olive oil within a few days. He was trying to ingest enough calories to make up for eliminating sugar. (It sounds so gross, but the smoothies were actually somewhat tasty.)

Eventually, Josh settled on a Paleo diet. By then we had found it was easiest if Josh prepared his own meals while I catered to Justin and Carter. It was a relief finally not having to continually cater to Josh's ever-changing diet plans. To be honest, I don't like to cook. My Mom always says she regrets not encouraging me more in the kitchen as a kid.

Two weeks after Josh started chemo, he was quite impressed that he hadn't lost any hair. Needless to say, the very next day, after scratching his head, he noticed that some came out. Rather than being alarmed by the concept of losing his hair, he kept pulling at it, fascinated that more kept coming out. The next day while showering, his pubic hair fell out all at once.

Sunday, July 19

Over the weekend, the hair on his head became patchier and patchier. I gently encouraged him to shave it and offered to help him with it. He agreed that the rest needed to go, but he wanted to do it by himself.

I was sitting on the back deck relaxing and thinking about our new normal when suddenly he appeared—sans hair.

It shook me to my core.

My husband had always had a thick, full head of hair. He

had always looked healthy and strong. Seeing his bald scalp shattered me. This was real. I was now faced with the undeniable evidence that my husband, my Superman, was not infallible, and his body was showing the effects of the poison that was targeting his cancer. I quickly excused myself and went for a walk. I had to get away from the reality. I needed time to process. Josh was always logical and relatively unemotional. I couldn't talk to him about it, not just because I didn't want to be upset in front of him, but because I knew his perception was much different from mine.

As I walked, I ran into two neighbors, Heather and Leslie. They saw that I was in distress and pulled me into Heather's backyard to talk beside her peaceful pool. They were deeply concerned and allowed me to share. I felt safe to release some of my anguish. I sobbed, trying to make sense of the intense emotions that I was feeling. I had never faced anything like this before. I didn't have a compass of a similar experience to draw from. After I cried and let out some of the grief, my burden lightened a bit, and I was able to return home, ready to love on my family and acclimate to my newly-bald husband.

Sunday, July 26

I went to church with the boys, as usual. I'd become accustomed to observing the many husbands and wives seated in the auditorium, listening attentively to the weekly message. I accepted my aloneness during those services, but often I felt jealous of the other couples and wished and prayed that Josh would join me. Not to just sit beside me and go through the motions, but to be fully engaged in the spiritual process with me—together, as a team.

In my heart, I felt that my husband would never let go of his skepticism enough to fully accept Jesus in his life. I continued to invite him to join me from time to time. The few times he came along, I'd be ecstatic. But then I'd be crushed to see him sleep through the service or hear him criticize the pastor's message. He'd also refuse to sing many of the songs. He said the lyrics were intended to brainwash people. It saddened and hurt me that

I could not share my spiritual life with him, but I had no choice but to accept his position. In truth, I felt I had to tamp down my own faith so we would not find ourselves on completely different paths.

On top of all that, our emotional responses to his diagnosis were completely different. Josh looked at his illness matter-of-factly and wanted to deal with it head-on as if it were just another project he was taking on at work. But I, the more emotional one, was devastated, knowing that my husband had a life-threatening disease that most people do not survive.

With that thought in mind that Sunday, I walked into the house, acknowledged Josh, and stood silently in our sun-drenched kitchen.

"Ange," he asked, "what's wrong?"

In my head, I screamed, *"Are you kidding me? You have to ask?"* But, I simply said,

"Josh, you have cancer, and everything is changing!"

"I don't understand," he replied. "Talk to me."

"I'm overwhelmed, and I'm emotional!"

"But, why?"

Why?? That's what he said! Really!

Really?!

In that moment, I realized, I'd never be able to go there with Josh. I couldn't share my fears with him. He didn't understand the heart-wrenching emotions I was experiencing, so he wasn't capable of giving me the emotional support I needed. But then I felt selfish. There I was, all emotional and needing support. And there was Josh, acting like he just had a condition that needed to be figured out and all would be well.

I couldn't be around him. I walked out onto the deck and bawled.

I decided that, for the time being, I had to refuse to give in to the "what if he doesn't make it" scenario. I wouldn't allow myself to go to that dark place and envision a future without him. I wouldn't allow myself to imagine what losing him would feel like or look like. I wouldn't allow it because I didn't know how to deal with it. So I locked away a vital piece of my psyche, deciding I'd consider the possible consequences some other time.

Tuesday, July 28

I accompanied Josh to his next doctor's appointment. I think he was apprehensive with me there—he wasn't sure how I would hold up emotionally, or how I would interact with the doctor.

Neither of us was prepared for the information Dr. Kotiah had in store for us. She told us she'd been rehearsing what she would say to Josh that morning. She already knew that he'd challenge her about his care. I loved Josh for all he was, but when he was determined about something and did his research, you'd better hope to God that you knew your stuff inside and out! Dr. Kotiah looked at us head-on. "Josh, the good news is that your tumor is shrinking. The bad news is that, as it shrinks, the hole that it created in your bowel might re-open, and you could become septic again. I need you to consult with a surgical oncologist because you might need a colostomy."

Say that again? A colostomy? A poop bag? I thought the chemo was doing its job!

She immediately took us to see the surgical oncologist, Dr. Vadim Gushchin, a no-nonsense man with a slight Russian accent, whose office was conveniently located just down the hall, in a medical building that was situated in a renovated Giant grocery store in Timonium, Maryland.

Dr. Gushchin did not sugar-coat Josh's prognosis. He discussed the need for a colostomy and what that would mean. Josh's biggest concern was that he wanted to have the 10 cm tumor taken out. He thought it would make him feel emotionally stronger if he could get rid of the mass that had already punctured his colon. But Dr. Gushchin advised that it would not be a good idea to perform more invasive surgery because Josh had already started a round of chemo, which could diminish his ability to heal. We agreed to trust Dr. Gushchin to perform the operation and decide what was best once he got into Josh's abdomen and could see precisely what he was dealing with.

Josh's surgery was scheduled for Tuesday, August 4. Coincidentally, that fell right in the middle the week we had already slated for vacation. We had been considering driving up to my hometown of Fairport, New York, for my 20th high-school reunion. So, not only was I off from work that week, we had already made other plans for Justin and Carter. My parents had started a tradition of renting a house for a week at Deep Creek Lake in Western Maryland and inviting the whole family to join them—my family and my younger brother's growing family. I knew that my kids and their four little cousins would be well entertained while I spent the week focused on Josh's needs.

Tuesday, August 4

We drove down to Mercy Hospital for Josh to have his surgery, completely unsure of what the outcome would be. Nonetheless, there was Josh, on his laptop, intent on finishing a project for work. I had made him wear a Mr. Incredible T-shirt to encourage positive vibes for a successful surgery. He put a coat over his head to shield his screen from the bright sun. I'm sure the other drivers were wondering what body I was hiding in the passenger seat. As we pulled into the parking garage, he continued to punch his fingers on the keyboard, determined to finish what needed to be done. Anxiety welled up in my chest as the minutes ticked closer to the time we had to check in for his surgery.

Maybe it's just me, but I can't imagine doing work right before an operation that could very well determine how long I might live. But Josh was a self-professed workaholic—or maybe I was the one who professed that. Josh's incredible commitment to doing a good job pushed him to finish. Thankfully, he finally hit the send button, and we went inside. He checked in, and we waited to be called back.

I walked with Josh back to the pre-op room and watched as he gowned and got ready to roll for his surgery. We met again with Dr. Gushchin to go over our treatment options and priorities. He made it known that he wanted a minimally invasive procedure to re-route Josh's intestines, potentially insert an ostomy, and then possibly remove the tumor. The good doctor made it clear in no uncertain terms that being more invasive could have disastrous consequences. But Josh wanted to be in charge of his care, much to the occasional frustration of his healthcare team. He, in turn, made it clear in no uncertain terms that he felt great, was ready to take on the surgery, and wanted the tumor *out.*

With everyone's arguments duly noted, I anxiously returned to the reception room to await whatever outcome would be. As I sat there, I prayed fervently for Josh. I also tried to meditate to calm my nerves. Our dear friend Sarah, who worked nearby at the University of Maryland Hospital as a doctor of physical therapy, graciously showed up to wait with me. She chatted sweetly to me about life, the kids, work—anything to keep my mind busy while we waited for the news. But the most important thing she said to me that day was a gift I will always treasure. She told me simply, "Josh loves every molecule of you."

After what seemed like many hours (it was less than two), I was ushered back to speak with Dr. Gushchin. His serious face did nothing to abate my anxiety. I took in a deep breath and waited. "Well, your husband got his way," he said. Then he drew a crude picture of a bowel and showed me that he had resected (cut out) parts of Josh's small and large bowel. "It was a mess in there with pus and adhesions. I had to take out some of the small and large bowels that were stuck together. I also removed the tumor. He does not have an ostomy."

Praise God! Breathe out....

The doctor continued, "I hope that he heals from this. It was more invasive than I wanted it to be. I tried to go in laparoscopically, but it was too much, so I made an incision down his abdomen. He'll be recovering in the PACU. The nurse will let you see him as soon as he wakes up." Relief overwhelmed me for a moment, and I could feel the adrenaline shoot through my body as I realized that Josh got exactly what he wanted from the surgery. I felt that he was going to be absolutely fine! I couldn't wait to tell him the good news. After another agonizing delay, I was allowed to see my dear husband.

As soon as Josh's eyes fluttered open, I gushed out the good news. However, I didn't get the response I was anticipating. "It hurts so bad," he whispered. "What does?" I asked. "The incision? The abdomen?" I looked for the nearest nurse, and she administered more pain medication. He couldn't indicate what hurt, and he kept squeezing his eyes closed, as if the effort might help block the pain. Finally, we were escorted into his hospital room, a surprisingly spacious, inviting room that had a beautiful view of the city of Baltimore below.

Normally smiling and positive, Josh grimaced in distress. Most of the pain was caused by the catheter tube in his penis. His pain medication came from a locked box that he could administer himself. When he pushed a button, a dose of meds shot directly into his veins. But he wasn't allowed to administer it more often than, I think, every six minutes.

All night long, Josh waited for those six minutes to push the button. As I have mentioned before, he was not one to complain. So, when I saw he was living for the next button push, I could only imagine how excruciating it was for him. Not to mention he'd had a 7 cm tumor taken out (the chemo had reduced it by 3 cm), a part of bowel removed, and multiple incisions in his belly, all adding to his distress. It was a long, painful night for him and a fitful night for us both.

Wednesday, August 5

When morning came, I could see that his discomfort had eased up a little. He was able to sleep in short intervals, in spite of the constant parade of nurses that came to check on his vitals and administer various meds.

I like to think that by being by Josh's side those few days, I was helpful to him. Honestly, it gave me a sense of being needed. I could not magically eradicate the cancer from his body, but I could fetch things he needed and be his support as he walked gingerly around the hospital floor to regain his strength. Once the catheter was removed, he remarked that he felt surprisingly well. Then we began the wait for his bowels to start working.

After sustaining trauma—like having a chunk removed!—bowels don't want to work for a bit. We'd been waiting two, long days for them to wake up when one of the nurses did a "poop dance" for Josh, a goofy shimmy of sorts to bring humor to the whole situation. Unfortunately for her, Dr. Gushchin walked in at the same time and made a wry remark about her lack of professionalism. I think he was secretly amused.

Friday, August 7

Three days after surgery, Josh's bowels woke up. It sounds funny to be so focused on that and to celebrate it so much. If you have ever potty-trained kids, you know how exciting it can be once they figure out how to do it correctly. I felt like I had won the lottery when Justin did it for the first time, years before. I had a similar feeling of elation when Josh finally found success in the bathroom.

At that point, Josh looked at me and said, "Ange, I want you to go to Deep Creek Lake and be with your family." At first, I refused. How can I leave my husband? How can I leave this man who is going through the biggest challenge of his life? As I worked through the guilt of all these questions in my head, I realized that Josh wanted me to do something that would make me happy and allow me to step away from the harsh reality of perpetual illness. It was a beautiful gift, and I decided I'd receive it. I also thought he was ready for me to stop hovering around him so he could get some work done and sleep quietly whenever he wanted.

The next morning, I headed to Deep Creek Lake, under a brilliant, sunny sky. I was enjoying the quiet drive alone when I realized that I was in desperate need of a hug from my Mom. I needed to be surrounded by someone who loved me and had always supported me. I surprised everyone with my arrival and basked in the love that instantly enveloped me. Sometimes I take having a loving family for granted and fail to fully appreciate the beauty of it. But not that morning. I cried silently and let my parents and brother wrap me up in hugs. As the stress of the week started to melt away, I felt the weight lift from my tired shoulders.

I hadn't realized how much I'd been pushing forward since July 1, putting on a sunny smile, trying to be unceasingly positive, while still refusing to indulge in the "what if" questions and scenarios.

I took those two days and engaged with and loved with my family. They created a safe haven for me to lay down my burden. I released the tension and truly lived in the moment with my parents, my brother, his wife, their four adorable girls, and my two wonderful sons. On Saturday night, we went waterskiing. As I glided through the invigorating water, I praised God for being alive.

The boys had been having a blast all week with their cousins, aunt, uncle, and grandparents. They'd been doted on all week and did not show any distress from worrying about their Dad. I saw that they were concerned, but it didn't keep them from *living*. They were such a beautiful example of living in the moment, not worrying about what was to come but enjoying what was right in front of them.

We drove home the next day, a Sunday, not knowing what kind of life awaited us. But for the time being, we felt that our cups were full, and our batteries were somewhat recharged. Josh's parents had kindly picked him up and brought him home from the hospital. The boys, ecstatic to see him, understood that Dad was in a delicate condition and that they shouldn't jump all over him like they normally would. But Josh engaged verbally with the boys as he always had, asking them about their vacation—what they did and what their favorite activity had been. (It was tubing—they loved being tossed about in the waves behind the boat.)

That week, we fell into our new routine. Josh worked from home, and I went back to my office, grateful to take care of people and feel like I was making a difference somewhere since I felt helpless to extinguish Josh's cancer. The kids happily went back to enjoying the day camp in the park near our house. Meanwhile, Josh's incision had healed beautifully, without complications. Dr. Gushchin was genuinely surprised that he was mending so well and determined that Josh could resume chemotherapy in a couple of weeks.

In mid-August, our youngest was turning 9. He wanted a party at SkyZone, an indoor trampoline park 30 minutes from home. It featured multiple trampolines that allowed for ample jumping and flipping—a great outlet for the energy of young kiddos. Each of our boys had come to expect certain birthday traditions and routines, and I felt it was important to continue them. But while I agreed to the party, I wondered how Josh would manage it. He was recovering from his surgery with a 5-inch vertical incision in his abdomen. I knew that he was not about to be jumping around on the trampolines with Carter and his friends. Then my brother, Dave, and his wife, Lauren, called to say they'd decided to drive up from Virginia with their four little girls—the youngest just two months old! I was so touched and grateful.

I drove Carter, Justin, Josh, and a few of Carter's friends to the indoor jumping park. Josh settled in one of the many massage chairs at the foot of the steps leading up to the trampolines. He was such a trooper, slowly moving from chair to chair, then trying to rest a bit within the chaos of the environment. I knew he wanted to be a part of Carter's party, and I was happy for that. But it was stressful for me, running back and forth, checking on Josh, then chasing after a bunch of very energetic boys, making sure we didn't lose anyone. But Carter had a blast, and I knew that by going ahead with the party, we had done the right thing.

Miraculously, Josh breezed through the ensuing chemo treatments into September, joking that he'd been given fake chemo. He continued to observe a Paleo diet and run regularly. He drove himself to and from his chemo appointments, while still working and engaging in other activities.

I remember being surprised—but not really, knowing Josh— that he met Sarah for a run one day after a chemo treatment. He often said that he wasn't tired and felt well enough to run. I trusted him, mostly, but I worried at times that he was doing too much. I didn't want him to get run down and succumb to the secondary challenges that cancer and chemo can create. But I knew in my heart that he was going to get through this round. I was certain that he was going to beat the odds. Because he was my Superman. I clung to that and pushed all negative thoughts out of my head (well, at least I shoved them to the deep, dark recesses of my brain and locked them up tightly). Maybe I was unrealistically optimistic, but it was the only way I was able to support my business, run the kids where they needed to be, and care for my husband when he needed it (which was not very often).

One day I mentioned to Josh that we should take a trip, just the two of us. I wanted to go somewhere we hadn't been before. Even though I was very optimistic about the future, I didn't want to wait to travel. We only have this moment that we're in—just right now. Why wait? After much debate, we decided on Spain.

We discussed with Josh's oncologist our plan to go overseas. As one might imagine, Dr. Kotiah was less than thrilled by the idea. I mean, who goes over to a foreign country, while undergoing chemo, especially when your white blood count could plummet at any time, making you vulnerable to infection? Josh does! The doctor agreed that she would release him to go, but only if his white blood cell count fell within an acceptable range. It did.

We decided on a week-long stay in Spain at the beginning of October. I started to hash out an itinerary, while Josh began researching places to stay. He continued to feel well, although, once again, he was experiencing some discomfort in his upper belly. I wasn't sure if it was partly apprehension about going overseas while having health challenges or if something was starting to grow again. Dr. Kotiah ordered a CT scan to make sure we were in the clear. Sure enough, no new tumors were discovered, and the four spots they had found on his liver in July were gone, too. Encouraged by the good news, we nervously began our adventure overseas.

Friday, October 9

Our journey began at the airport in Philadelphia. I dropped Josh off at Departures, then went to find a place to park my Ford Explorer for the week. When I met up with him again at the ticket counter, he was grumbling about my over-packing. Not only was he not a big fan of packing heavy, I hadn't realized there is a

50-pound weight limit on some airlines, and I had exceeded it significantly. Ever frugal, Josh was determined to avoid the extra cargo charge, so he was frantically moving shoes and toiletries into other bags to redistribute the weight. I think the attendant took pity on my bald husband and accepted my suitcase at 54 pounds. Admittedly, I was a little ashamed for packing so much, given the gravity of our situation. It really hadn't been necessary to pack those extra two pairs of shoes....

After sitting for seven hours, our flight finally landed in Madrid. We grabbed a rental car and headed east to our first stop, Barcelona. It had only been two days since we had made the final decision to leave for Spain, so we hadn't made plans beyond our first destination. I drove as Josh stretched out in his seat beside me, trying to relieve the discomfort in his abdomen, his body protesting the prolonged sitting.

Saturday, October 10

About midday, we arrived in the heart of Barcelona known as the Gothic Quarter, a trendy but very old region of the city with great eateries and many architectural wonders to explore. We had decided to use Airbnb to book our accommodations, not realizing that the apartment we'd rented entailed a six-story climb up a narrow stairwell—there were no elevators. Josh insisted on carrying my 54-pound bag up every flight, the whole way chanting to himself, "I love my wife, I love my wife." Guilt flooded me as I watched him slowly lug my suitcase up the steps, but he absolutely refused to let me help. All I could think was, *"What am I to do with this man?"*

At the top, we were rewarded with a fantastic view of the city of Barcelona, including the tips of the spires of La Sagrada Família Basilica. Then we investigated our apartment. We were in awe of the New Age feel of it. The entry room was like an empty box with its sides adorned with a variety of different sizes of colored rectangles and squares. When you pushed on one of the shapes, it would open up to display the room within. We discovered the sink and kitchen behind one of the larger panels. I loved Barcelona already.

Whenever Josh and I traveled together, the first thing we'd do is explore the place on foot, and the next day was no exception. We walked all over the city, checking out the small pebbled beach and many of the old buildings.

Spain is mostly a Catholic nation. I am a Christian but not Catholic. However, at every Catholic church we visited, I made sure to say a silent prayer for healing and sprinkle holy water on Josh. I meant no disrespect to Catholics. I just wanted to shower Josh with anything and everything positive, and I figured some holy water couldn't hurt.

The next day we visited La Sagrada Família, which was begun in the late 1800s and to this day remains unfinished. "Wow" is the best word to describe the awe-inspiring architecture of this incredible structure. As Josh and I entered the sanctuary, I was amazed by the very high, almost alien-looking ceilings and the intricate stained glass that appeared to have real water flowing out of it. The walls were smooth and inviting. One wall featured a prayer in 50 different languages, welcoming all into its embrace. We walked the halls and climbed up into the ornate turrets. All the while, I prayed fervently for Josh's recovery.

Although man-made, this beautiful structure felt otherworldly. I felt God's presence there. Every aspect of this church had been created to glorify Jesus and his life. But more than that, it focused on love and acceptance. I felt a sense of peace there I had never felt inside a building before. I felt that God was speaking to me, making me feel that He is always with us and that we are loved. No matter what the future holds, we truly are not alone.

I felt peace for a while that afternoon. I couldn't control the destiny of my husband's future health challenges, but at that moment I rested in Him and knew that no matter what, all would be well.

Barcelona was so engaging, we decided to stay for three nights. Meanwhile, we figured out where we'd go next. We chose Valencia, a lovely city that sits on the coast of the Balearic Sea.

As soon as we arrived there, we walked and walked, discovering the sites, including the city's beautiful aquarium.

Unfortunately, throughout the trip, we couldn't help feeling unsettled, knowing that something could change in an instant. At night, Josh would gently massage his belly, which was still causing him discomfort. It made me uneasy to think something could be growing in there. And yet, each day we pressed on for miles, exploring the surroundings, and enjoying each other and the sweetness of our companionship. We had been together nearly 20 years, and even in silence, we found comfort in each other's company, like a warm blanket surrounding us both.

One particular challenge, however, was finding suitable meals. Josh was still eating a Paleo diet, which means very few carbs. Eating in a country that has bread, rice, wine, and delicious pastries at every corner was difficult for him to navigate. I just told him that I would happily drink his wine and eat his dessert. All joking aside, uneasiness followed me every day as we searched for appropriate meals.

After two more nights, we headed to Madrid to take in the Museo Nacional del Prado, a world-class museum with an astounding assortment of art treasures. However, for all its diversity, I instantly recognized that the most frequently recurring theme was of Jesus on the Cross. The image struck me as especially powerful, just as we were navigating the most challenging chapter of our lives. As I gazed upon the depiction of a love so great and transcendent it can overcome anything, I experienced a sense of peace more profound than I ever had before.

From Madrid, we decided to take a bullet train to Segovia, a small town 60 miles away, to visit one of the ancient world's best-preserved aqueducts. Built by the Romans more than 2,000 years ago, this engineering marvel stands as an incredible testament to the craftsmanship of the Roman Empire. It has withstood the test of time and the elements, even surviving Europe's ruinous, war-filled history. And yet, there it stood in its well-preserved glory for us to admire. I found the aqueduct an excellent metaphor for life: We all have our battle scars. Some are visible on the surface but, more often, they are hidden deep in our hearts. We, too, withstand the tests of our own time, and yet we keep going. We keep rising each day to take on whatever life has in store for us. We carry with us, in the fabric of our being, our story, our hurts, our joys, our scars, our loves.

I discovered that when you take a trip away from home, you relax. I know—not a big newsflash—but it was such a treat to enjoy one's husband without being constantly pulled in a million other directions. I could completely focus on the man I had married. We enjoyed moments of laughter as we figured out how to navigate the foreign cities. I am, by default, directionally challenged, which was always a source of amusement for my family. I could even get disoriented in familiar places. Josh, however, apparently had an internal compass, and, together, we never seemed to get lost.

There was one episode on the trip, in Valencia, when Josh's discomfort had increased to the point that we agonized about whether we should go home to be monitored. Josh was afraid that the cancerous tumor would grow back and puncture his bowels again, causing even worse havoc than before. But in the end, I felt the trip was a success in that Josh had remained healthy all week. I was glad we'd taken this special time to enjoy each other's company and discover new places. We were still on this journey together, in sickness and in health, whatever that might bring.

Sunday, October 18

We ended our beautiful week-long trip overseas and flew back to Philadelphia. A fluke snow squall greeted us on the drive to Josh's parents' house to pick up our precious boys. They'd been so busy with school and activities they'd barely missed us. It was such a joy to come home from a long journey and wrap our arms around our children.

After spending a few days at home recovering from our trip, we met with Dr. Kotiah. She looked at me sternly when we admitted that Josh had walked at least 10 miles each day. But actually, I think she was impressed by his stamina. I insisted that Josh had been quite capable of the activity, and I knew that he felt better

41

when he walked every day. It boosted his energy and helped him mentally. Dr. Kotiah did not change his treatment plan, so Josh resumed his regular chemo routine, three days on every three weeks.

Josh never allowed himself to be a "cancer patient." He carried on as if he were healthy. That was his *modus operandi*. I knew that his determined positivity was keeping his cancer at bay.

One day in early November, Josh mysteriously asked if we could take the kids out of school early on November 20 so that we could enjoy a special, surprise family trip. I racked my brain to figure out where we were going and what he was up to. His only hints were that it would be warm, it would take 2 to 6 hours to get there, and it would be just for the weekend. He refused to tell us anything more, even on the day of our departure.

Friday, November 20

That Friday, we collected our children early from school and started driving north for a couple of hours. Clearly, we weren't going to an airport, so why were we heading north where it is definitely not warm, especially in November? As we hurtled along the highway, the boys and I eventually saw a building ahead that had large, colorful tubes sticking out the side of it. "Is that it, Daddy?!" they asked excitedly. Sure enough, our destination was a brand new resort, with a 100,000 square-foot indoor water park, in the Poconos of Pennsylvania. The boys were beyond excited once they understood what this beautiful resort held in store for them.

We spent two days swimming and riding the lazy river and water slides. It was incredible spending time together as a family. We enjoyed just being in the moment. Josh climbed all the stairs and went on all the water slides. I idly wondered what Dr. Kotiah would think of him, in the middle of chemo treatment, playing in a warm environment with who-knows-what floating in the water.

Monday, November 23

The next day, back at home, we celebrated Josh's 40th trip around the sun. I thought it was strange—40 used to sound like such an "old" age. But, after coming face-to-face with cancer, it now seemed incredibly young—a vibrant age—a time to appreciate life's entire journey, the part already lived as well as the part yet to come.

As it was almost Thanksgiving, we planned to have a party of sorts that following weekend. I asked Josh how he would like to honor this birthday. This year, he told me, he just wanted to celebrate with a home-cooked meal, surrounded by family. Josh was never one to be the center of a celebration. I knew that a big bash was truly not what he wanted, so I respected his wishes and suppressed the urge to throw a big shindig.

Tuesday, November 24

Upon our return, Dr. Kotiah ordered a PET scan to see how Josh was progressing after six rounds of chemo. On Tuesday evening, Josh and I were walking into Justin's 5th grade parent-teacher conference when the phone call came in with the test results. Josh looked at me when he hung up. I nearly hyperventilated with anticipation. Finally, he shared, "They can't detect any cancer from the scan. It's clear." I was so overwhelmed with gratitude, I felt giddy. Being the realist, Josh followed up with, "Ange, this doesn't mean it isn't there. It just means that the test can't detect it." Being the optimist, I replied, "I don't care. Right now, you don't have detectable cancer, and I'm going to celebrate!"

I blurted out the good news to Justin's teachers as we proceeded to get an excellent report on his progress that year. Justin didn't like to talk about his Dad's condition at school. Nevertheless, his teachers had been kept abreast of our home situation, and now they rejoiced in our news. Justin was blessed with an incredibly caring team that year. They showed genuine interest and concern in how he was doing. He loved his teachers as well as going to school and doing "normal things."

Thursday, November 26

The morning of Thanksgiving Day, the four of us celebrated by running in a 5K Turkey Trot in York. It had become a family tradition for us, and this was our 4th year taking part in the race. It was an unusually warm day, and we reveled running with our children. I ran into a number of friends from the local gym, where I had previously taught group fitness classes. I excitedly shared the news of his latest scan, while Josh shook his head at me. He didn't want us to get ahead of ourselves, knowing the cancer could return at any moment. I didn't care. My feeling was that we had looked cancer in the face and told it to go to hell. At that moment, it wasn't running rampant in his body. And here we were, a mere five-and-a-half months after getting the scariest of all diagnoses, running a 5K as a family. And Josh was very much alive and fully capable of participating in this event.

Josh, being more patient than I am, stayed behind to run with Carter, our younger son, while I trotted ahead with Justin. We ran down streets with 5,000 other people, cheered on by local residents and family members. It was a celebratory run for me. I was still high on Josh's good news, and for the moment it felt like we were in the clear. It was thrilling!

A couple of days later, the families—his parents, my parents, and our brothers and their families—celebrated Josh's birthday with homemade chicken salad and lots of veggies to adhere to his strict diet. The rest of indulged in some homemade cookie cake, but Josh, always good-natured, assured us he didn't mind at all. That was another admirable trait. Josh never harbored resentful feelings or acted as if life was unfair. Never once in the face of his cancer did he complain, "Why me?" He had met it head-on and thrown all he had at it, doing everything he could to help his body beat the odds.

Because Josh's diagnosis was so aggressive and he was managing so well with the chemo, the doctor decided he should have two more rounds to make sure the cancer was at bay. Just as before, Josh continued to breeze through the additional treatments with a smile on his face. He threw up a couple of times during each of these rounds, but otherwise, he responded favorably.

As his company's chief information officer, Josh worked particularly long hours during the winter holidays, preparing W-2s and wrapping up all of the year's loose ends. Many times in the past, I would anxiously wait for him to meet us at church for the Christmas Eve service, but he was always late. Occasionally, he didn't come at all. But this year, uncharacteristically, he showed up on time, and we were able to enjoy a special service together as a family. I sang the traditional celebratory songs of Christmas and basked in the happiness of having my family together.

That Christmas Eve in church, I noticed something different about Josh. He seemed more engaged in the celebration of Jesus's birth. Not only did he stay awake for the service, but he was also fervently singing and smiling. I have a picture of him picking up both boys, who at the time were 65 pounds and 110 pounds. He looked so strong, capable, and joyful. In my eyes, he seemed happily invincible.

Although the chemo had done its job suppressing the cancer, Josh asked to be given a new immunotherapy drug called Opdivo, which had just recently come on the market. It was supposed to help his body kill cancer cells. He had researched it completely and was happy to be following an additional course of treatment, while continuing to maintain his healthy diet, exercise program, and sleep regimen. Dr. Kotiah worked her magic and was able to get our insurance company to pay for the new treatment. So Josh kept going to the medical center in Timonium to have the new drug infused for 90 minutes, every two weeks. He didn't notice any side effects and, with the holiday season behind us, we continued to enjoy our regular lifestyle. Josh was still going to work, the boys were doing well in school, and I was growing my practice. Josh had made significant changes in his life, and I was happy how he had modeled this beautiful way of dealing with the scariest of diagnoses. He wasn't working as many hours and was sleeping more, eating clean, and feeling happier.

I remember Josh commenting that if he were around for our

25th wedding anniversary, he was going to give me an anniversary ring. Jewelry was not a gift that I often received from Josh. He didn't see much value in it. In fact, besides my engagement ring, I had only received one other piece of jewelry, a beautiful, heart-shaped necklace from him. So, when he offered to give me an upgrade for our silver anniversary, I was all too happy to hold him to it!

Late that January, we were blessed (I chose to look at it that way) with 30 inches of snow. The four of us hunkered down and watched the flakes fall for hours. Needless to say, we were snowed in. The boys were tremendously excited and took every opportunity to go outside, dig tunnels, and play with their neighborhood friends. Meanwhile, Josh snowblowed our driveway many times. When the snow stopped, we were grateful the plows came through our neighborhood. Some other places didn't get plowed for five days!

Josh thought it would be a great idea to go skiing at Roundtop, a small mountain 25 miles away. We all chipped away at the last of the snow in our driveway and made the arduous drive to Roundtop. Josh was excited by the idea of skiing on powder. If you've ever skied in the eastern states, you know that natural powder is a rare occurrence. We made it and enjoyed a day navigating 30 inches of fresh powder. We only lost one ski, which we later found buried in the snow. It was an incredible, sunny, perfect ski day, and the four of us thoroughly embraced it.

As January turned into February, Josh planned a trip for himself and our youngest, Carter, to go skiing in British Columbia. The previous March, Josh had taken Justin to Utah to go skiing for a long weekend. Given all that he had just gone through, he didn't want to wait any longer to take Carter on a similar trip.

The two journeyed to Canada and met up with Sarah and her fiancé, Chris. Carter was thrilled to be on an adventure and have all of his Dad's attention. I received a text shortly after they arrived, which said that Carter had not brought a winter coat with him (it was always a struggle to get him to wear one). It pained Josh to shell out $200 for a new one, but wisely, he chose a warm, brightly colored coat that would be big enough for Carter to wear the next season. Josh patiently went down slopes with Carter as he negotiated the harder western terrain and snow for the first time. Josh told me that although Carter had struggled with the *big* mountain, he had successfully managed all the others. They shared many special moments together, hot tubbing outside and eating pot pies. While they were away, Justin and I enjoyed a quick overnight ski trip of our own to the Poconos.

It is such a special treat to have one-on-one time with your children. It happens so infrequently, but when it does, you get a glimpse of who your child truly is and start to see who they might become. Both of our children showed such appreciation of their time with us. Of course there were challenges and grumpiness, but only occasionally and always short-lived.

In spite of some challenges, Carter and Josh returned with huge smiles on their faces and countless little stories of their adventures. Carter, with his sunny disposition, happily chattered away about how much fun he'd had with his Daddy.

For a while, I was lulled into thinking that we were back to normal, back to being the four of us, as we had been before cancer wreaked havoc in our lives. I started to believe that cancer was behind us, and we had dodged a massive, devastating bullet. We could relax a bit and release some of the worries that had been dogging us for months. I started thinking more about our future and imagined where we might take some trips together, as a family. It felt like we'd returned to our pre-cancer life.

And yet, in the back of my mind, I was rather disappointed to find we were slowly falling back into our old routines, the same ones we'd followed before Josh got sick. I didn't *want* us to be the same. I didn't *want* us to go back to where we were before the cancer diagnosis. I wanted to think that we had evolved into something better because of our experience. I wanted to think that we were wiser, more connected, and more committed to our family time than ever before. I felt that God had given us this challenge for a reason, and I didn't want to squander or ignore it.

I wanted to see it as a gift—an opportunity to make changes for the better.

But slowly I could see Josh getting sucked back into working longer and longer hours, and I, too, was following my same old schedule, running the business and raising our kids. Our experiences hadn't changed anything. I didn't want to go back to that place. I wanted to be evolved, forever and for the better, to be a better person, wife, mom, friend....

CHAPTER 6

The Fight for Life

In late February, Josh began to notice some discomfort and bloating in his abdomen again. Another CT scan was scheduled to determine what was going on, but he couldn't get an appointment until March 3, the day we had planned to drive to Vermont for a ski trip with some of Josh's fraternity brothers and their families.

March 3, 2016

Josh drove down for his test, and I got ready to open my office for a short while before leaving later in the day. I remember chatting away with my best friend, Erica, that morning. I was wishing her a happy birthday and telling her how happy I was that things were going so well and how amazing Josh had been through all of it.

That afternoon, as we sped north toward our destination, we received the call. "Josh," said Dr. Kotiah, "we got your results from the CT scan. You have a large mass in your omentum and pelvis, as well as others in your abdomen. I'm so sorry."

Josh answered calmly, "I understand. We're on our way to Vermont. Should we come back now or just enjoy the weekend?"

"That's up to you," the doctor replied. "Let me give you my cell phone number in case you need anything. We can start another round of chemo on Monday when you return."

"Are you okay to drive, Ange?"

I had to focus intently on the road in front of me as tears poured down my frozen face.

"Yes."

"Do you think we should turn around?"

"Yes and no."

We drove for another 20 minutes. Then Josh started texting Dr. Kotiah, asking her whether it would be best to start chemo again right away. The boys in the back seat were much sobered to hear that their Dad's cancer was back.

Josh was considering his two choices when Dr. Kotiah texted to say that, because the cancer had come back so quickly and was all over his abdomen, it would be best to start chemo without delay. At this point, Josh looked at me, and I knew. We needed to turn around. We were just outside New York City. As I crossed over to the right lane to get off at the first exit, the boys began to cry, recognizing that we weren't going to make the ski trip after all. They understood why but were unable to disguise their disappointment. We drove a bit farther then stopped at a gas station. Justin and I got out to use the bathroom. As we were finishing up, my 11-year-old looked at me, then asked me pointedly: "How long does Dad have?" That surreal feeling washed over me again. "I don't know," was all that I could offer.

Not once had I let myself think that Josh would actually succumb to his illness, and I still wasn't ready to think that way. We *must* have other options. He kicked ass in his first round. Why not this round?

We arrived back home exhausted and in shock. After tucking the boys in for the night, we climbed into our bed and held on to each other, cherishing our precious quiet time together and bracing for whatever was next in store for us.

Friday, March 4

In the morning, we sent the kids off to be with their grandparents and headed down to Mercy Hospital to start a new round of chemo. Because it had been less than six months since Josh had been off of the Cisplatin and Etoposide, he would have to adopt a new protocol. We were quite familiar with Mercy by now, so we settled quickly into his new room and waited for a new action plan. Josh, always restless, decided to do pushups. He did *42 in a row*. I gazed at him, amazed that while cancer was running rampant in his body, he maintained the ability and strength to push his body up 42 full times. After everything he'd been through, he was still my Superman, proving his ability to show strength even in the hardest of times.

At last, Dr. Kotiah came in and outlined our new game plan. Josh would start on a round of Fluorouracil, Oxaliplatin, and Irinotecan. She mentioned that sensitivity to cold might become an issue. It seemed laughable because Josh was always warm. I recalled a time in college when he stood outside, barefoot in the snow—in just his underwear—for a full half hour, never shivering or showing any ill effects.

The nurses accessed his port, and his infusion commenced. Never once did we discuss "What if...." We focused on the new regimen and remained hopeful for an outcome similar to the one the previous fall. By the time he was discharged on Sunday, he felt that the tenderness and discomfort in his belly had diminished. Dr. Kotiah noted that as well.

When cancer reaches the omentum (the apron of fat that covers the abdominal organs), it is very difficult for the chemo to impact the cancer cells adequately. In the course of his research, Josh had read that high doses of marijuana could potentially have positive effects in the reduction of cancer. Josh never wavered in his commitment to try just about anything and everything and take any possible opportunity to chance a cure that might rid himself of cancer. With recovery our only concern, we acquired some medicinal-grade marijuana and decided to try a protocol that studies indicated had been helpful to some people.

Sunday, March 6

We arrived home on Sunday. And because we had planned to be gone until Tuesday, I didn't have to worry about going to work the next morning. With the kids away at a friend's house, Josh decided it was a good time to try a dose of medical marijuana and ingested what he thought was a reasonable amount. Then we went straight to bed, exhausted from the emotional weekend. Sleep, however, was not in the cards for us that night.

Josh didn't smoke pot, and he was unfamiliar with its effects. Nor did he know what a typical dosage was, certainly not in liquid form. Consequently, he orally ingested *the equivalent of 25-30 joints*! For someone entirely unaccustomed to pot, it slammed him hard. Within an hour, he was experiencing paranoia and decreased muscle function. He could barely stand, even with support. I had never been around someone under this much influence, and I didn't know what else to do but seek help. So we decided to go to the ER, back at York Hospital. At this point, he could barely speak coherently and was struggling to breathe. I couldn't tell if he was having a panic attack or suffering the effects of such a high dosage.

We arrived at the ER late that night. When Josh told them his breathing was impaired, he was quickly escorted back. I told the nurse about what had happened but tiptoed around the topic of marijuana. A medicinal marijuana law hadn't been passed yet in Pennsylvania, and the last thing I wanted was to deal with the law on top of everything else. She understood me and discreetly explained the situation to the doctors in the ER.

At some point, a resident came in the room to check on Josh and very unceremoniously began examining his abdomen. With a belly riddled with cancer, Josh was very sensitive to deep palpation, and this fledgling doctor was utterly unconcerned about the discomfort he was inflicting on my totally-stoned husband. Josh winced many times while the doctor, in a flip manner, asked him what was going on. Josh, always sharp-minded, answered slowly and thickly. The doctor kept questioning him in a patronizing tone as if he were addressing a toddler. He completely dismissed the reason why Josh had gotten himself into this position in the first place. It was insulting to all the challenges he had faced. I was incensed that this young doctor showed no sympathy for this life/death sentence Josh had been handed and showed no appreciation for how serious his condition was.

Throughout our *lovely* stay in the ER, Josh kept repeating to me that he was going to die and that he was so sorry. I assured him that he was *not* going to die that night. He just had too much marijuana in his system. His body was trying to detox while, at the same time, it was absorbing the chemo he'd had earlier that weekend.

The attending doctor finally paid us a visit and kindly told Josh that there was nothing they could do—he would just have to wait it out until his body flushed out the effects of the THC. He said it could take 24 hours, but then he'd be fine. So, after being poked and prodded but feeling no better, we headed back home.

As we climbed the stairs, I gently supported Josh's shrinking frame. He had started to lose weight again. Back in July, when this all began, he had weighed nearly 200 pounds. Now he was 175. I coaxed him back to bed, but he rested fitfully, waking up often with anxious notions of impending death.

Monday, March 7

The next morning, he had made no improvement whatsoever, so I decided to call Dr. Kotiah. I explained the situation, and she offered to give us a referral to the infusion center in Timonium. She thought fluids might help flush the THC out faster.

Meanwhile, our friends graciously offered to keep Justin and Carter longer than we'd originally planned. Thankfully, the boys were kept occupied, having fun with the other kids. Once again, we headed for Timonium.

Josh, still unsteady on his feet, allowed me to get a wheelchair to take him back for an infusion. As I have already said, Josh was always independent. So, when he gave in to using a wheelchair, I knew exactly how horrible his pain must be. The nurse on hand, who had usually given Josh his infusions that past year, knew immediately that he was nowhere close to himself. He was still slurring his speech and was extremely sluggish. After 30 minutes of rehydration into his port, his nurse encouraged us to go back to Mercy and have the doctors re-evaluate him there.

I dropped Josh off in the waiting room at the ER at Mercy and explained to the attendants that he was still in a mostly incoherent state. I made sure he was stable in his wheelchair, then went to park the car in a place where it wouldn't be towed. As I walked back to the ER, I reflected on the past few days and shook my head at the craziness of our weekend. My mind refused to absorb what we'd experienced these past few days.

Meanwhile, I had been in contact with Karen, our dear friend and Josh's colleague at his workplace, which was only 15 minutes away from the hospital. She desperately wanted to visit and asked if she and a couple of other people from work could stop by. I didn't think I should allow his co-workers to see him in this state. I was pretty sure that Josh, had he been coherent, wouldn't be too happy about it. Nonetheless, they all showed up at the hospital, so eager to show their support for him. I was grateful for their love and care, but after they said a quick hello to Josh, I encouraged them to go home and promised to let them know once he was in a better frame of mind.

Karen stayed for a while, then ran off to get us dinner. I couldn't remember the last time we had eaten. Karen was a godsend, quietly giving us what we needed without asking for anything in return. Just as I was reaching my very limit, she went and got us some food. And then she hugged me.

It had been such a long weekend. But I continued to refuse to give in to the powerful emotions that were lurking just around the corner. I did not have the luxury to stop and give in to the tears that were always so desperately close to the surface.

Eventually, Dr. Kotiah paid us a visit in the ER and ordered an MRI to rule out that the cancer had not spread to Josh's brain, as his speech was still slurred and he was still mentally sluggish. At this point, it had been more than 20 hours since he'd ingested the liquid THC, and he hadn't improved significantly. One of the ER docs, also a toxicologist, told us it could take as long as 36 hours for the THC to clear his system. As an extra precaution, Dr. Kotiah graciously ordered Josh to be admitted for the night for observation. He was woozy but didn't complain. He was just grateful to get some sleep. Meanwhile, his MRI came back negative.

Before this all happened, I had scheduled my normal Monday patients to be seen on Tuesday because we had planned to be skiing in Vermont. Now, with Josh back in the hospital, I knew I wouldn't be able to treat anyone anytime soon.

One of the downsides of being the only chiropractor in your own business is that, if you don't work, you don't get paid. I wanted to keep my office running, but my husband needed me. Reluctantly, I reached out to my staff to let them know that I wouldn't be able to see any patients on Tuesday, either. Pam, my office manager, decided to reach out to fellow chiropractors in the area to see if they could spare a couple of hours to fill in for me. Miraculously, all of my hours were covered by two generous friends and colleagues, Dr. Jim Sheaffer and Dr. Selina Sigafoose. I felt honored to be taken care of, on so many levels. It re-affirmed my belief in God, and how He always has our back, no matter how dire or trying a situation.

Tuesday, March 8

On the third day, I was greeted by a much more clearheaded husband, who had spent another night at Mercy. Josh was finally able to enunciate clearly and speak coherently, and the paranoia had finally abated. He continued to get fluids until the nurses and doctors were finally satisfied the THC was no longer at work. They released us in the early afternoon. I was grateful to have my husband back, with all of his faculties.

I had been in caregiver mode all weekend—something that I was more than happy to be for my dear, sweet husband. But I needed a break. For the moment, knowing that Josh was okay and functional, I wanted to direct my attention to something that did not make me think of cancer and prognoses and chemo and side effects and uncertainty. I decided I'd go into the office. Josh was used to taking care of himself, and we both needed space to do other things. I felt I had to relieve my friends, who were voluntarily taking care of my patients that day.

I work with patients and teach them how to achieve optimal health by getting adjusted, eating right, exercising, thinking good thoughts, and immersing in healthy relationships. I focus on wellness. And if you do all the right things, you're not supposed to get sick, right? I knew how to adjust my patients and often advised them of ways they could take better care of themselves. Unfortunately, no amount of advice could rid my husband of his cancer.

Just one year before, Josh had been running marathons. After his diagnosis, he still ran 3-5 miles a few times a week. He ate well and slept more than the seven hours a night that studies now recommend. How could cancer have invaded his body? In both our families, people lived well into their 90s. Every single one of our grandparents had reached old age, and our parents are still alive. We'd never had to deal face-to-face with such things as aggressive cancer and dire prognoses. We had no compass for that. All we could do was try to stay optimistic and live every moment to the fullest.

As I walked into my office, I heard a colleague taking care of one of my patients. I was relieved to know they were in good hands. I have been so fortunate to have a job that I love. I've met many wonderful people and have been surrounded by a team that always has each other's back. I was able to keep my doors open that day and catch up on other work demands.

After our harrowing weekend of emotions and physiological challenges, we now had to start a new regimen of chemo. Thus began Round Two in the effort to kill this cancer. Josh appeared to be responding to the chemo, and the discomfort and distension that had returned were starting to ease up with this new round. As he began to feel better later that week, he slowly started going back to work.

We decided that if he were to try medical marijuana again, it should be in much smaller doses so that he could work his way up, in levels. One day, later that same week, he went out for lunch with his brother, Jake, and sent me a picture of them eating outside. Josh had a very doped-up look on his face, reminiscent of our weekend experience. I replied it was too soon for me to see that face to find it particularly funny. I was still nursing the rawness of our past weekend.

Josh started experiencing some of the side effects from the chemo we'd been warned about, especially an intense response to cold. He felt electric-like shocks in his hands any time he reached into the refrigerator or washed them in cool water. It was weird to see my usually warm husband walking around with gloves on. I started making his smoothies in the morning so that he wouldn't have to handle the bags of frozen fruit. Anything I could do to help him made me feel useful.

The month progressed, and Easter was almost upon us when dear friends of ours, Mark and Brenda, called to say they wanted to visit us—along with their six boys, ages 7 months to 12 years! I loved the idea of seeing them but was overwhelmed by the thought of housing a family of eight. But Josh seemed excited to have them come and stay with us. We hadn't seen them in nearly four years and missed them dearly. Several years before, after the birth of his fourth child, Mark had been diagnosed with non-Hodgkin's lymphoma and had gone through chemo and all that it entailed. Thankfully, he had been in remission ever since and gone on to father two more children. Mark wanted so much to support Josh and take him to chemo.

Friday, March 25

A couple of days before Easter, our loving friends pulled up in their extended Nissan NV. As you can imagine, a lot of energy surrounds six boys. And when you added in our two, it was pandemonium. But what was so beautiful was that all of the boys immediately engaged with each other. They thoroughly enjoyed playing with friends they hadn't seen for many years.

Amazingly, having our friends stay with us that week was a huge blessing. Yes, there was chaos. But Mark and Brenda were good at corralling the boys and keeping them busy, so they were no trouble. It was a pleasure to have them stay with us.

Mark took Josh to chemo one day, and they followed it up with a trip to the gym. Mark commented on how strong "chemo boy" was. Josh was still pushing himself to keep strong, and he was able to lift a significant amount of weight. I think that psychologically it helped him feel better and offset some of the less-than-pleasant side effects of the treatment.

One evening that week, Mark took charge of the kids so Brenda and I could go out for a girls' dinner. I would finally be able to voice my concerns with another woman who'd already experienced and gotten through her husband's cancer diagnosis.

I sat at the small table in one of my favorite restaurants, with delicious hard ciders and gourmet food spread out before me. I looked openly at Brenda and felt the emotions I'd kept locked in my heart start to break through. I began to feel the *depth* of my pain. I was grieving that my husband's body was no longer healthy—it had been invaded, and our future was uncertain. But, still I wasn't able to discuss any possibility that Josh might not survive this. I loved this man. He was a part of me. To even consider that he might not pull through this was unthinkable. I was, however, very willing to express my feelings of being overwhelmed. The ability to communicate my grief was a true gift. I was grateful for the bond that Brenda and I now shared. No one wants to be a member of the cancer club, but it was comforting to have an informed friend who was willing to listen to me. Brenda gave me the compassion and opportunity to let the tears flow.

As I spoke, could tell from the expression on Brenda's face that she had considered the "what if Josh dies" scenario. She had dealt with those "what ifs" years before. I saw the worry in her eyes, and I knew she was wondering how I would manage our future without Josh. Still, I wouldn't go there—not with her, not with anyone. I was determined to remain positive.

I focused on what needed to be done and carried on as if Josh would pull through. We would go on with our lives as if nothing changed. That was my focus, that was my mantra, that was all

I could think about. Avoid considering any other outcome and push forward. Never mind that my husband had a deadly type of cancer that almost no one had survived. Never mind that his body was getting weaker with this round of chemo. Never mind that he could actually die, and I could be a widow. Never mind that this wonderful man could physically leave this Earth, and my children might be fatherless. Never mind that I might go to bed alone and wake up alone. Never mind that I might never kiss this man, or go on dates, or laugh, or get mad, or make love to him again.

Winter formal at Cornell University in Ithaca,
New York, December 1995. Our first date and
already in love. We looked so young!

Before the illness: Josh and Justin skiing in Utah, Easter 2015.

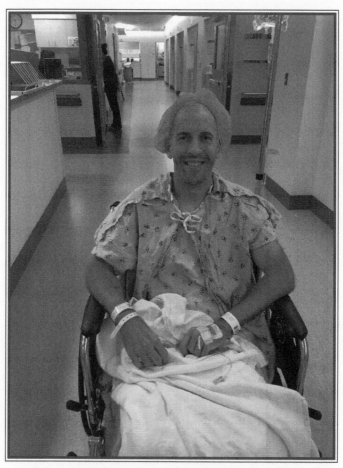

Josh all scrubbed and gowned for his
abdominal surgery, August 4, 2015.

Josh and me on the coast of the Balearic Sea
in Valencia, Spain, October 2015.

Josh and Carter enjoying their special father-son ski trip in Whistler, Canada, February 2016.

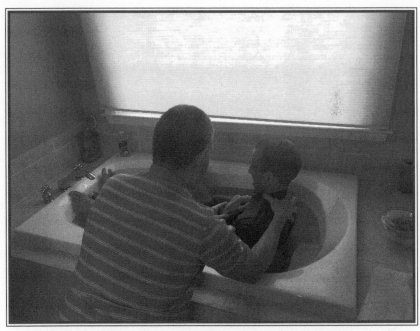

On April 22, 2016, less than three weeks before he died, Josh was baptized at home in our soaking tub.

The Mother's Day flowers Josh gave me on May 8,
2016, just a few days before he passed away.

Father and son: Josh and Justin embrace in a beautiful final hug on May 10, 2016, just one day before Josh's death.

On June 23, 2016, six weeks after Josh died, I received these flowers from him on what would have been our 15th wedding anniversary.

Our sons, Justin and Carter, in June 2016, sitting on the park bench we built for Josh. Incredibly, one month after their father's death, they still found a reason to smile.

Have you ever felt constrained? Have you ever felt like your whole being has been stuffed into a box that's too small for you? Looking back now, I'm astonished at the amount of crap I had to tamp down and shove into the far recesses of my mind. That's a lot to keep hidden away. That's a lot not to acknowledge and work through. I'd held all those fears at bay. It had been more important to focus on the present with Josh and to engage in the *now*. Whatever the future held, I would avoid crossing bridges until I came to them.

That strategy worked, at least so far as keeping the household running relatively smoothly. The boys followed our lead and put their brave faces forward to tackle each day. Carter was playing soccer that spring, so I would spend a couple of evenings a week getting him to and from practice. I felt bad that I never stayed to watch because I would have to run errands or start dinner and such. Justin was involved in lacrosse at the same time. I was fortunate to have a compassionate neighbor who knew of our situation and offered to shuttle Justin to and from his practices with her own son. I missed a lot of their games that spring, caring for Josh and trying to keep things moving smoothly at the house. Jake, Josh's brother, and Zeke, his Dad, were always there that spring to support both kids' games. On the weekends, they would show up to cheer them on. I was so glad that the kiddos had other family members to fill in and represent us. Neither Justin nor Carter ever indicated they needed to have a cheering section at each game. But I know deep down they appreciated having the support, especially with all the uncertainty they faced at home.

At the beginning of April, Josh started showing signs of ascites, a buildup of fluid in the abdomen that was causing more swelling. We knew it wasn't a good sign and rushed off to meet with Dr. Kotiah. She and Josh ended up having a heated discussion about his treatment plan. Both thought they were right, and I, always eager to avoid conflict, just wanted to leave the room. They finally agreed on a new strategy. Meanwhile, Josh had to go back to Mercy to have the fluid drained from his abdomen.

The next day, I went to work and Josh's parents took him down to the IR department at the hospital. The procedure relieved him of six liters of fluid, equivalent to over a gallon and a half! They stopped because to take more out meant he would have needed an infusion, and he was done being in hospitals at that point.

Over the next couple of weeks, we continued this cycle a few more times. Josh would go down to Mercy to have fluid drained from his abdomen, and then he'd return home, only to have his belly fill up again. It kept happening more and more frequently. Finally, the doctor suggested that Josh come down and have a drain permanently placed.

The week before, Josh had found a holistic practice in Fairfax, Virginia, that specializes in helping cancer patients. We drove down to see what options they could give us. They discussed Vitamin C infusions and a host of other interventions. The doctor had been straightforward about the options and potential outcomes. He said he could start Josh on a different chemo regimen that would use a lesser amount but potentially be more targeted. But first, we needed to touch base with our current doctors. We left the consultation and considered the options.

Tuesday, April 12

Again we found ourselves at Mercy, this time to have Josh's drain placed. We both thought that it would be a quick outpatient procedure. Some fluid was released—not as much as before but enough to give him some relief. Then we were ushered upstairs to be monitored and have bloodwork done. The results showed that Josh's sodium levels were low. The doctors decided to keep him in the hospital while they tried to balance his sodium. Tuesday turned to Wednesday, Wednesday to Thursday, and Thursday to Friday. Josh continued to take his supplements and observe his Paleo diet.

Friday, April 15

On her Friday rounds, Dr. Kotiah stopped in Josh's room to discuss his status. She looked him squarely in the eye and chose her words carefully. "Your sodium levels are not rising. We are out of options at this point. I'm so sorry, but it's time that we talk about end-of-life procedures. Do you know of a hospice company in York?"

Josh looked at me. I finally broke and released the dam of tears. This wasn't happening! How could this be? We had never even thought about hospice. That was for really old people! Josh was only 40! My only experience with hospice was through my grandparents, and they had been well into their nineties. NO!! *This can't be!!* But the world of medicine had nothing left to offer us. We were released from the hospital to go home and prepare for whatever we were supposed to endure.

No one at the hospital in Baltimore had known of any hospice companies in York. So I had to call a friend, a nurse, to see what was available in our hometown.

"Heather, it's Ange. Um...I need names of hospice companies...."

I couldn't continue. I had reached my absolute limit. My mouth would not form any more words. I handed the phone to Josh— who calmly continued the conversation.

They say denial is the first stage of grief, and I was way in it, real deep. We had become BFFs, and I'd have been happy to stay camped there—forever if I had to.

Josh and I agreed to invite a chaplain over to visit so we could pray together. A lovely woman with a soothing voice came and prayed with Josh and me. In his calmness, I noted that my husband was ready to endure the next step with even more remarkable grace than he had already shown.

Remember the woman I mentioned earlier, Gloria, who had counseled Josh to pray, right after he'd been diagnosed? Josh had been following her advice and had started praying daily. He then told me that, around this time, he'd started hearing a voice that was not his own, and that he attributed his incredible fortitude and endurance throughout his ordeal to God. I never, *ever*, thought I would hear my wonderful husband, a skeptic of all things, utter that statement. I embraced the words that the chaplain shared with us that afternoon, and I clung to His solace as Josh and I faced what appeared to be our last steps together.

I texted my friend Jennifer and asked if she would pick the boys up at the bus stop and keep them until the next morning. We needed time until we were better equipped to talk to them about what was going on with their Dad.

Josh, who had been so strict with his diet all year, asked if I'd go to Potbelly to get him a juicy meatball sub. I was more than happy to comply. That was *something* I could do.

Two of Josh's dear friends from his fraternity, John and Seth, had planned to come by to visit that evening. Josh didn't have anything contagious, he wasn't leaving us at that moment, and he could still ambulate, so we decided to follow through and meet our friends at a restaurant near our house.

After 5-10 minutes of sitting, Josh asked to go to the car. We all quickly packed up our food and went home so Josh could sit comfortably, and the four of us could catch up. John and Seth stayed with us for an hour or so that night, chatting about what was going on in all of our lives. Josh was frank about his situation but conveyed an undertone of hope. All hope was not lost. He was still here—but for how much longer, we couldn't know.

Several months before, Josh and I had purchased a TV console for our home. It had taken us five years to find a piece of furniture we could agree on. While we were at the furniture store, Josh had happened upon an enormous massage chair that was equipped with all the bells and whistles. Light therapy, soft wraps for your hands, and slots to put your calves to be massaged were just some of the features of this crazy piece of machinery. It also came with a crazy price tag.

That afternoon, Josh asked if we could go to the same store and look at the massage chair. I was more than happy to comply, so we took off to inspect it again. Watching my frugal husband eye this massage chair was unbelievable. The fact he was even considering it made me grasp how desperately uncomfortable he was. After a significant amount of encouragement from me, he reluctantly let me buy it for him.

That night, after hearing the worst news of our lives, Josh settled himself into the Cadillac of all massage chairs and fully engaged in conversation with our friends, smiling all the while. But after a time, he was obviously exhausted and excused himself to go to bed. I joined him shortly, and we clung to each other, but thankfully we fell asleep quickly. We'd done enough processing for one night.

Saturday, April 16

The following morning, our friend Jenn dropped Justin and Carter off at the house. They ran inside, leaving me alone with her for a moment. We hugged each other, and I told her what had transpired.

Josh was lying in bed upstairs. I asked the boys to go up with me and join him. The time had come to tell them their Dad's news.

"Boys," Josh started, "the doctors can't do anything more for me. I'm going to be meeting with hospice so that we can have help."

"What does that mean?" they asked.

How could these two little boys begin to digest any of this, I thought, *when Josh and I barely could?*

"It means that Daddy's cancer is overtaking his body," I said, "and we are running out of options. We don't know how long he will be with us. There is always hope, though, and we will keep praying for a miracle. But we wanted you to know things aren't good right now. We both love you so very much."

As their little minds absorbed the information, grief washed over both their faces and they started to cry. All four of us held on to each other. We held on for dear, sweet life. We held on for Josh. We held on for each other. We held on because we were afraid to let go—afraid that if we did, Josh would disappear.

That was one of the most powerful experiences I'd ever had—telling our children that their Dad might not be alive in the near future, while crying and holding to each other. At that moment, I felt our souls make a pact with each other. We would never let go, we would never be far from each other, even when our physical bodies let go of life. It gave me a sense of peace that convinced me we would persevere, with or without the miracle we were desperately praying for.

Shortly after that, a cheerful lady from hospice arrived, and all five of us sat down in the family room to consider our options and current needs. As we started to get into the nitty-gritty details, the doorbell rang, and our 16-year-old neighbor stood on our doorstep, offering to play football with the boys. What a gift! The boys gladly went out to play, taking a break from the heaviness of life to be boys and be free for a few precious moments.

Josh was still self-sufficient in his self-care, and because I was strong and healthy, we determined we wouldn't need a lot of services just yet. We agreed to have a chaplain visit us regularly, and a nurse would check in and make sure that Josh was comfortable. The hospice worker shared some of her insight on what to expect and suggestions about what to do. She advised Josh to write letters to the boys and such. Even if he were to pull through, she said, we would always have a record of his thoughts during this time.

I remember Justin coming in later that day, having spent most of it outside. "Mom, I feel bad going outside and having fun and leaving Dad." Reassuringly, I told him, "Justin, I'm so glad you can go out and play. Enjoy this beautiful day. We can spend time together this evening."

Word got around quickly that Josh was not improving, and a dinner brigade ensued. Apparently, a very thoughtful person created a Sign-Up Genius and started recruiting volunteers to bring us dinner most nights of the week. Cooking, as I have already said, is not one of my passions in life, so I was especially grateful.

Over the past year, I'd been entertaining the idea of hiring an associate for my office so I could grow the business and help more people. I had been meeting monthly with a young chiropractor named Dr. Sam. He was considering leaving his current employer, but he had signed a contract to stay on through July 2016. I kept in touch with him all through 2015 and the beginning of 2016. I'd been sure from the start that I would hire him eventually.

And then my life changed, and here we were in April 2016. I didn't want to miss any time caring for Josh, so I asked Dr. Sam if he could get permission to help out at my office. I would never have asked had circumstances been different, but I was desperate. I decided I'd ask people to fill in for me in the mornings, and I would work three afternoons a week. I thought this would give me a change of pace and would also give Josh's brother and his parents the opportunity to sit with Josh some afternoons, giving them precious alone time together.

Thankfully, Dr. Sam's employers allowed him some time off to help me, and I was able to find another person, a professional "coverage doc," that could fill in the rest of the holes. So our new routine ensued: The kids would go to school, and I would be with Josh in the mornings and some afternoons. Josh, always one to follow through with his commitments, did a little bit of work to occupy his mind and make him feel productive on some level. It was really special to have him home after so many years of commuting 40-miles away and working really long hours.

I felt guilty admitting this to myself, but it was a relief to take a break from cancer by going to the office and taking care of patients. I will say, though, I'd definitely lost tolerance for people who'd whine about little things. I kept it to myself, but it made me angry when a patient would complain about their husband because he hadn't done something or that they had a painful hangnail. Seriously? My husband is at home dying, and you want to complain to me about that? I love my patients, but at times some tested my patience to the very limit.

One afternoon that first week in hospice, Josh texted me, "Do you still have a pastor friend? I was thinking I'd like to have an at-home baptism, or at least take Communion."

Say, *what??!!*

The previous weekend, Josh had confided in me that he truly believed in God and that Jesus died on the cross for our sins—that he was all in. I really couldn't believe it. After all those years of going to church by myself and not being able to fully share my belief in God and Jesus throughout our whole marriage, now he was getting it? I once said that I felt God had given him cancer so he could be close to Him. Josh had joked, "Because I'm stubborn?" *Um...yes honey, you said it....*

I am privileged to count several pastors among my patients, and miraculously, the perfect one, Pastor Don, came into the office that afternoon. I asked if he would be willing to come to our house and baptize Josh. He instantly agreed, and we decided to do it the very next day.

Friday, April 22

At 9 a.m., Josh—surrounded by our kids, my parents, Josh's parents, and my brother—was formally baptized in our soaking tub at home. He went under the water and came back up, all smiles. He felt amazing and showed more energy than he had in days. I quickly began to hope that, since he had experienced the miracle of faith, perhaps his health might improve. He said he felt "different" and was grateful to Pastor Don for coming over to perform the ritual.

That weekend, Josh said he wanted to go to church. I had never seen him express such enthusiasm before, and I was overjoyed by his newfound commitment and eagerness to get closer to God. Josh desperately wanted to take Communion. Our church only offered it periodically, so I went in search of one that could fulfill his request.

Sunday, April 24

Our friends Rick and Amy attended a non-denominational church nearby that offered weekly Communion. Josh mustered the energy, and we trundled off with the kids and his brother, Jake, in tow. He appeared relaxed and grateful to take part in the ritual and said he wanted to do it again, as often as he could.

Friday, April 29

The following Friday, Josh and I had a date while his parents generously took the boys overnight. Our date was a stay-at-home one, but we enjoyed each other's company. Josh sucked on oxygen, and I folded myself up on the nearby couch. He asked for a Guinness beer, something he hadn't indulged in for nearly a year. Guinness was his favorite, and he slowly savored the dark drink.

Later that night, we climbed the stairs to bed and enjoyed a special intimacy that I didn't think was possible in the late stages of cancer. We made love that night, with a gentleness and connectedness unlike any other time we had ever experienced.

Josh exuded an incredible peace during this time. He was content, and, when he wasn't napping, he would spend time reading the Bible. He was using a lot of oxygen throughout the day, and our walks outside now consisted of a tenth-of-a-mile, down the street and back. He would carry his little oxygen tank, and I would follow him with a wheelchair in case he got too winded. He never sat in it. He would always push himself to the stop sign before he'd go back.

Around this time, my brother, Dave, had the wonderful thought of asking Josh questions and recording the interview. For 40 minutes, Dave asked him about his thoughts on politics, what advice he had for the kids, his feelings about me, and what words of wisdom he had for his parents and brother. Josh lay in bed, enveloped in his orange track jacket, waxing philosophical as he calmly assessed his life. He shared his thoughts with exuberance and love. It is a beautiful documentation.

It was hard to imagine that, as his body was slowly breaking down, Josh was able to convey and share so much peace. I always thought that when someone was dying, they would be grumpy and everyone around them would be miserable all the time. At least, that's the model we usually see in the movies—people standing around, crying. But whenever anyone visited Josh, they'd leave with a new understanding and appreciation of life.

There were lots of tears, but there was also much beauty.

Even though Josh was disappointed that he wasn't getting better, he was joyful. He never showed bitterness towards his situation. Only once did he get choked up about his own condition. He would get emotional for us, but never for himself. Once he said he'd noticed our new washing machine had a warranty of 10 years, and that it would most likely outlive him. Sometimes it's the little things that bring us face-to-face with our mortality.

Justin started asking to come home early from school, and we indulged him that first week in May. Josh was able to play a few video games with him, and they enjoyed that special time together. Because their life at home was constantly changing, I had tried to keep Justin and Carter on a regular routine. Every night, Josh would lie down with them and talk about whatever they wanted. He would take extra time to be with each of them as they contemplated space, math, reading, and life.

Pastor Brian paid us another visit that week. Josh was very tired by then but expressed gratitude for the visit and prayers. Then Pastor Brian and I had the surreal conversation about what a funeral for Josh would look like. He gave me some things to consider, such as how long it would take to get it together and what funeral home to use. Not a conversation I wanted to have, but it gave me an understanding of what to expect. I felt like I was talking about someone else. Someone else was dying, and we were talking funeral arrangements for them. Not Josh. I think I was only able to talk about it coherently because Josh was still alive, sitting beside me. His living body was sitting next to me on the couch. Again, my mind would not accept the full depth, let alone the reality, of the implications of our discussion.

Later, Josh shared further instructions for me. He told me that if, or when, he died, I shouldn't drown my sorrows in wine, or get so wrapped in my own grief that I'd neglect the needs of our children. He also cautioned me that if, or when, I became involved with another man, I should not share my financial situation with him until we were engaged. Josh was very private about our finances. He always wanted to live simply, regardless of how much was in the bank. This had allowed us to save money, and it gave us both peace of mind in the face of an uncertain future. He fully expected me to find love again and assumed I would attract someone relatively quickly. This was yet *another* surreal conversation. I had been with this man since I was 19! To contemplate having another man in my life seemed unimaginable. But there he sat, matter-of-factly, explaining his thoughts and reasons. He clearly wanted Justin, Carter, and me to have a future filled with joy and success, whether he was with us physically or not. I don't know how he did it so calmly, without emotion. I couldn't imagine being able to speak so coherently or having the same conversation with Josh if our positions had been reversed. He continued to show up as superhuman in his ability to be completely thoughtful and altruistic. Not once did he wallow in self-pity or complain about the unfairness of it all. Instead, he focused on the people most important to him. To me, that was ultimate love. Jesus demonstrated the ultimate sacrifice, and there was my husband giving us the gift of his unconditional love.

Sunday, May 1

The following week, we attended our regular church, another non-denominational, that plays amazing music and radiates a positive message. That day they were performing a healing ritual. Elders of our church stood at the front, available to offer prayers for anyone in need of healing. With Josh in his wheelchair and with his oxygen tank, we made our way to Pastor Steve, who offered us a brilliant prayer for healing, peace, and the presence of God.

After rounding a corner, we happened upon Pastor Brian, who also offered his prayers and let us know that he would be available if we needed anything, which brought me to tears with gratitude. I wheeled my husband back to our seats and held his hand as the service continued.

Then...he looked at me. "Ange, this might be the last time I make it to church." The floodgates opened up again, and I let myself grieve. I clung tightly to my husband's hand.

A couple of days later, with Josh's consent, I reached out

to Pastor Brian and asked if he'd be able to visit Josh at home so he could take Communion. Sure enough, despite his busy schedule, he said he'd be more than happy to come over. He sat and listened as Josh shared his journey with cancer and ultimately his faith conversion. The good pastor sat there, stunned by Josh's incredible calm and acceptance, which he interpreted as a sign of God's hand in our lives. "You are quite unusual in how you are handling this, Josh. Many people would be upset and bitter, but you are handling this very differently. That is incredible." We shared in Communion with the boys, and Pastor Brian prayed for us. He left after an hour and promised to come again.

Josh would always push himself to walk every day. It gave him a chance to stretch his legs and also relieve the pressure in his abdomen from the fluid that was only minimally relieved by the drain. That evening we took a stroll around the block, and he was able to complete the 0.7-mile loop with relatively little windedness.

I took charge of his permanent drain. I checked it daily, changed the bandages, and released the fluid that had built up in there. When we saw that less and less fluid was accumulating in the collection bottle, we started worrying that there might be a blockage. One evening, our friend Sarah stopped by with Trish, her stepmom and a nurse, to examine Josh's swollen abdomen. We were trying to figure out if we should go back to Mercy to have it checked again. Josh wanted to exhaust all possibilities, so we agreed to go in, hoping perhaps the drain had just shifted position.

The next day, we went into IR again. Trish sat with me while we waited for the docs to do their thing with Josh. Finally, a kind doctor came out of the examination room. He gently explained that the cancer had created honeycombed pockets that were preventing the fluid from reaching the drain, making it virtually ineffective.

Without an outlet for the fluid, Josh started to experience significant swelling in his feet. He was having a lot of discomfort from the stretching of fascia and skin. Still, he never once complained. When the swelling in his legs and feet started to become unbearable, Josh decided to put small punctures in the tops of his feet, hoping to release the pressure. I felt torn as I watched him make a small incision into each incredibly swollen foot. Fluid poured out of both sides, and he felt some relief from the pressure. Unfortunately, once he'd started doing it, his feet continued to leak all the time. I'd constantly be putting towels around them to absorb the unending stream of fluid.

At the end of the first week in May, we resorted to getting a bed for downstairs. Josh was no longer able to climb the stairs, and he was struggling to keep any food down. I would hear his stomach growling as his body slowly consumed itself. But he would just look at me and smile, and we would share a wordless moment of connection. He kept a bucket next to his monster massage chair and would periodically spit up into it. He was subsisting on ice chips and sips of water.

We both were oddly fascinated by how rapidly the greedy cancer in his abdomen was changing his body. His muscles were atrophying, and he steadily lost strength. I had to start helping him shower, something he tried to do every other day. As I washed his emaciated body, I was shocked at how his once muscular body had withered so completely. But I was glad to have any opportunity to help him. Josh never seemed to need help. He always took responsibility for himself.

Sometimes I had wondered whether he really needed me in his life at all.

Saturday, May 7

It was on this Saturday night that Josh calmly looked at me and said,

"Ange, I think I'm done."

He had endured so much in the ten months leading up to this point. His body was clearly failing him. I had to help him go to the bathroom and get him from the chair into bed. He allowed himself to lean on me, and I would snuggle under his arm to give him the added strength he needed. His speech was weak, and sometimes it was hard to hear him, as he had to take deep, heaving breaths to talk.

Even though I could see he was slowly cleaving from this Earth, I kept moving forward, not letting myself think about any future I might have to endure without him. I would not give in to it. He had told his family that I wouldn't be alone for long. I couldn't fathom such a thing. I was still waiting for a miracle that he would live.

Sunday, May 8

Then came Mother's Day.

I was startled to hear the doorbell ring on a Sunday. I opened the door to the sight of a beautiful arrangement of flowers in a purple pitcher with a card attached. I immediately recognized my husband's chicken scratch. The card read, "Happy Mother's Day Ange...."

Let me reiterate something about Josh. He was always very sweet to me, but buying a lovely bouquet of flowers from an actual flower shop was way out of the ordinary. So, when I received this beautiful Mother's Day gift, I ran to him and threw my arms around him in immeasurable gratitude. The thoughtfulness was incredible.

That afternoon, my parents stopped over to be with us for a few minutes. Josh talked with them about how he was so impressed with Karen, our friend and his work colleague. He told them how she was so quick to do a great job, how much joy she had added to the workplace, and how she had been such a good friend to us. My parents had only met her once and were surprised to hear how deeply grateful he was for her friendship. Karen and her sister, Sarah, had made frequent trips up from Baltimore to sit with him and help me with dinners and the boys. They were so loving and easy to be around. They were very low maintenance. What I mean is, they didn't expect us to entertain them, and they brought such a feeling of peace when they would come visit.

That Mother's Day evening, the boys and I pulled up chairs and tray tables and huddled around Josh's chair to eat a takeout dinner from Panera. The sun slanted through the slats of the window treatments as we enjoyed our meal and precious time together as a family of four.

Monday, May 9

Sunday bled into Monday, and Josh got progressively weaker. It took so much effort for him to talk. I had already decided that I would not return to work that week. I wanted to spend every moment with Josh. I selfishly wanted all of him. I wanted every opportunity to care for him, to take care of all his needs. I'd been given this gift to help him, and I was ready for the task. He made it so easy for me. He was always smiling in gratitude and let me bring him his ice chips and change the towels around his feet. He had transitioned to using a porta-pot that weekend, and I was able to help him use it.

Tuesday, May 10

On Tuesday, Justin came home from school early to spend time with his Dad. He was anxious and kept looking at him worriedly, especially as his breathing became more labored. He would curl up with blankets and quietly sit close to him. Usually, Justin was always into something, so to see him content just to sit still and be quiet was such a difference. That afternoon, I captured a photo of Josh and Justin that is one of the most moving images I have ever seen. Josh's long, wasted arms, enveloping his eldest son in the most loving embrace imaginable. His son is leaning into him with acceptance of his Dad's fate. And with the knowledge that his Dad would not be with us much longer, he hugged him lovingly.

Josh started getting more and more uncomfortable in his chair. Sitting became painful for him. I placed a water-filled pillow under his backside that gave him a little relief. I thought he would sleep more comfortably in the mechanical bed in the living room, one room away from his massage chair. I was able to transfer him to the bed, but we struggled to find him a comfortable position. His abdomen had swelled considerably. I had weighed him a couple of days before, and he was 147 pounds. He was six-foot-one, and I was finding it more and more challenging to move him from location to location. But I was determined to do it by myself. I know I probably should have called hospice, but I wanted the sole responsibility for his care. That was my job—as his wife—in sickness and in health. I would sleep on the couch in the living room, listening to his breathing and wondering every night if it would be his last. I was determined, at all costs, to be with him when the end came.

Wednesday, May 11

The next morning, I found Josh extremely uncomfortable. I rushed to his side to help him use the commode when he signaled he needed to go. He sat on the edge of the bed and struggled to focus. Surprisingly, he reached up and lightly cupped my breast and smiled. I couldn't believe he could even think of doing such a thing in his condition. Nonetheless, I was happy to give him a reason to smile. He was medicated at this point with OxyContin to keep his pain under some level of control, and it was hard to follow the words that came out of his mouth. I decided to let Justin stay home that morning. He seemed desperate to be with his Dad, for whatever time he had left. Carter went off to school, I think to get a break from the harsh reality of what was going on at home. I promised to have someone pick him up early that day so he could spend some time with his Dad. My brother, Dave, had decided to come support us that morning and was on his way from northern Virginia. Josh's parents were also planning a stopover later that morning.

Josh was agitated and in discomfort, so I wheeled him over to his massage chair from his bed and worked to get him into it. With his excruciatingly weakened legs, I realized that I couldn't do it by myself. I couldn't get my husband placed in his chair. We stood in mid-transfer, unsure of what to do. I yelled for Justin to help, but his 11-year-old body wasn't ready to take on the awkwardness of helping his Dad into his chair. So I gently let Josh slide to the floor. I guided him into a sitting position on the carpet. I placed my body behind him and put my arms around him to support him. He could no longer lift himself up after so many days of not eating and little hydration, compounded by the medication. I asked Justin to call Zeke and Elise, Josh's parents, to see if they could come over quickly to help me move Josh. Thankfully, it turned out Dave was only a half-hour away, so I chose to be patient and appreciate these minutes that I could wrap myself around Josh. It had been hard to hug him from his chair, and now I was given this gift of time to hold onto him.

Everyone arrived around the same time, and we worked together to get Josh up and into his chair. When he finally got comfortable, we enjoyed a moment of peace and appreciation of each other's presence and help. After determining that Josh was settled, Josh's parents left, promising to be back at a moment's notice should we need them. Carter came home shortly after, and Josh's brother, Jake, came over as well.

Dave wanted to make sure that we ate. So, that afternoon, Dave, Carter, and Justin headed out to pick up food from the market. Jake and I decided to share a drink together. We tried to keep the conversation light as we sat near Josh, watching his chest rise and fall in an irregular pattern. I wanted to talk about superficial topics so I wouldn't have to acknowledge what was happening. I knew Josh wouldn't want us to sit there crying, so we tried our best to have a "normal" conversation—whatever that is. We sat there talking, and all the while I refused to think about what was coming.

Sometimes when Josh became restless, he would complain of a bad smell. I'm not sure why I chose this moment, but suddenly I rushed upstairs to grab an oil I used to help ease his distress. When I returned to the family room, Jake looked at me and tearfully whispered, "I think he's gone...."

I was mad! I was his wife! He was my love, my best friend, my husband, my world, and I wanted *all* of the lasts with him. How could I have missed his last breath! As my anger mounted, I looked at Josh—and he exhaled. I had been there, after all, to witness the final, peaceful breath that signaled he was finished with this life.

I buried my head in Josh's lap and bawled. I tried not to cry too loudly because I didn't want to frighten Jake. But, at that moment, I was in shock from the overwhelming loss. I felt my brain fracture into two parts—one aware of my surroundings and social cues, and the other in disbelief that life no longer animated my husband's body. With one last breath, I'd been rudely thrust into an entirely new life without the physical presence of my husband.

CHAPTER 7

My Life Undone

Jake called Dave and warned him about what had happened. He returned with the boys shortly after. Dave rushed into the house to see how we were. Josh's body remained in the chair, while we waited for hospice and the funeral home to arrive. I didn't realize this, but hospice has to come and do the official pronouncement of death. During this whole ordeal, Jake had had the presence of mind to look at the clock when it happened: 4:29 p.m., May 11, 2016.

I made my way to my brother's van parked out front to face my two sweet, boys. They were watching a movie, and I was reluctant to shatter their last innocent moment of enjoyment. How could I tell my sons that their Dad was no longer alive? I dreaded seeing their faces crumple in despair. I took a breath and shared, "Boys…I need to tell you something. Daddy's gone." They started to cry. "Do you want to see him?" I asked. I had no idea if this was appropriate for an 8- and an 11-year-old boy to see their dead father, but I wanted to give them the option so they would have closure, should they need it. Surprisingly to me, they said they did. We slowly walked up the front lawn and entered into what now felt like The Death House. And there he sat. I had a really hard time looking at him and registering that his chest was no longer rising and falling. *It couldn't be.* That chest rose and fell steadfastly for 40 years. Why did it have to stop? How can he not be alive anymore? *What is happening?*

Justin and Carter stared at him for a while, with sadness deeply etched in their young faces. I saw a layer of their innocence wash away as the realization of the loss of their Dad set in. I hugged them hard. Then Justin asked abruptly, "Can I go play on the computer?" At first, I was a little peeved by his heartless preoccupation. But I quickly recovered. He needed a break from this. He needed to focus on something mundane to slow down the processing of this unfathomable new reality.

Hospice arrived and pronounced Josh at 5:17 p.m. The nurse asked if we had any morphine or oxycodone meds left in the house. We had quite a bit, and she informed me that we needed to dispose of it. I was all too happy to comply—it gave me something to do, and, besides, I wanted the medication out of my house. She brought in a bag of kitty litter and dumped the meds in it. According to her, once you dump meds into kitty litter, it destroys the medication. I gave her all of his other prescriptions. I didn't want any of them around. I wanted to banish all signs of illness from my house. I wanted to think of Josh as strong and healthy, not dying and needing medication.

By now, Josh's parents had arrived. They had been so generous to give the last moments of his life to me. We had all been sitting, silently crying and figuring out how we were going to shoulder this grief when one of the directors and an assistant from Etzweiler Funeral Home came to move Josh. They carefully and reverently moved his lifeless body to the stretcher and zipped him up to secure him. They left his face unveiled so that we could all say our final goodbyes. Everyone had their moment, but I made sure I was the last to touch him. I was his wife, and I continued to want his lasts. I bent down and kissed his cool, hard lips. Those weren't the soft lips I had kissed thousands of times before. But I got the last kiss, the last touch, and the last word of love to my incredible man.

I was selfish. At that moment it was all about *my* grief. I was bereft and confused. Suddenly, my fractured mind remembered that the grass needed mowing. I texted my neighbor Kristin, whose son had graciously volunteered to mow it throughout the spring. I wrote that Josh had passed and that Kyle could mow now. She replied quickly, adding that it was the weirdest text she'd ever received. Admittedly, it seemed a bit insane to be focused on the lawn. But, at that moment, I wanted something normal, and I wanted the long grass to look nice. I wanted it to be mowed down. I wanted the long tips cut back. I wanted some action taken. I couldn't breathe life back into my husband's body, but I could fixate on the damn lawn. My mind wanted to focus on a to-do list, not on the loss of my beloved.

My brother took the initiative to cook dinner for us all that night. My parents, as well as Josh's parents, came around for a while but left shortly after the funeral home had taken Josh away. We all needed space to grieve in our own ways.

After dinner, Jake, Dave, Justin, Carter, and I watched *The Incredibles*, Josh's favorite movie. It was a relief to lose oneself in an animated world, at least for a little while. When it was over, Jake went home while Dave, graciously, stayed overnight with the boys and me. Thankfully, we were all able to suspend reality just long enough to fall asleep.

Thursday, May 12

When I awoke the next morning to an empty bed, I was struck with excruciating grief. As the tears surged, I allowed myself a moment to release the pain before getting up to face the day without Josh by my side.

I walked to the IHOP that morning with Dave and the boys, feeling a bit in a daze. That week had been rainy and overcast, but that day a glorious sunny sky gifted us with a reprieve.

Upon returning from breakfast, all I saw was the evidence of Josh's illness all over the house. I wanted all of it out—all of the hospital stuff that had invaded our home—the chair, the commode, the oxygen tank, and the hospital bed. I wanted all reminders of Josh being sick banished from our space. I wanted desperately to air out our house and rid it of the sense of death and illness. I wanted vibrancy and healing to return. I didn't want the boys to be constantly reminded of their Dad's illness. I wanted them to remember their loving Dad as he was before he got sick.

Always the planner, Josh had left a four-page document, outlining all the steps I needed to take after he passed. It became an incredible guide for me as I navigated that completely foreign land in which I was now living. It included whom to call after he passed, including hospice, the funeral home, Social Security, and the DMV to register his death status. It even had his obituary outlined in it. It was a well thought out list of the tasks I had to take on. I referred to it often, as I struggled to remember all the things that needed to be done. It was an incredible gift.

Josh's Dad, Zeke, and I had the unhappy duty of meeting with the funeral home that day to make arrangements. The funeral director was very kind and patient with us, slowly going through all the questions that needed answers to make the arrangements for Josh's Celebration of Life service: Cremation or burial? What type of paper for the service's programs? Would I want a necklace with his ashes in it? When and what time for the ceremony? And so on, and so forth.

Finally, he asked when Josh should be cremated. I knew that Josh's body was one floor beneath us as we talked, and it gave me a very unsettled feeling. I was so grateful to have Zeke there to be a source of strength as well as another tie to Josh. I was acutely aware of wanting Josh's parents to feel that I was honoring him in a way that reflected the man that he was and what he stood for.

Later that day, I decided to post on Facebook that Josh had gone home to Jesus. The monsoon of support and condolences that followed was staggering. Kind people sent beautiful flowers to help fill our loss. Our home became a flower shop. As the week progressed, gorgeous weather finally graced us with beauty after a wet and dreary spring.

Friday, May 13

Justin had been invited to participate in a Google-inspired day at the intermediate school, and he was torn about going. It would give him a break from the classroom, and he would have the opportunity to work on computers and problem-solving. I thought it would be healthy for him to focus on something completely different and something he loved. I dropped him off at school early that morning, two days after his Dad's death, with reassurances that I would pick him up immediately if he wanted to come home. Carter stayed home from school for the rest of the week.

Not only did Justin stay all day, he came home the proud winner of a white Google Chromebook. I said a silent thank you to Josh and instantly knew that it had been the right thing to send Justin off that day.

CHAPTER 8

Widowhood

I was a widow—at 39.

I knew of no one that I was close to that had been widowed at such a young age. Even now, I still grapple with the full reality of what that really means. Being widowed happened to other, faceless people. It didn't happen to people like me. People in our family live well into old age. No one died at 40. I was thrust into this closed box with no openings or hope for escape. This adjective, "widow," and all that comes with it, was placed upon me. I was the widow who no longer had the loving partner with whom I had spent the last twenty years of my life. Josh and I had been intimately connected for over two decades. We had grown into adulthood together—from college graduation, navigating first jobs, apartments, new cities, graduate school, building a business, marrying, birthing and raising children. We had shared so many firsts together, coupled in marriage and life. That doesn't just go away. Those bonds run very deep. I knew him, and he knew me, better than I did myself at times. Because he knew me so well, he'd had the incredible foresight and wisdom to leave me a plethora of gifts that would help me function and move forward in life without him by my side.

I had grief sickness. Just as a pregnant woman would deal with morning sickness, I had grief sickness. I would wake up, alone, and be instantly jarred into the new reality of being a widow. I would cry every morning at the loss of my spouse and the reality of being truly alone. I was quite accustomed to doing things on my own. I paid all the bills, was able to mow the lawn, trim hedges, run kids everywhere, manage a business, and all the other countless tasks and chores women do every day. I was capable. But I was not prepared for the being alone part. The I-am-all-by-myself-day-in-and-day-out part. Even though Josh worked a lot, we always touched base with each other. There were times he would spend the night at work so that he wouldn't have to commute the 80-miles roundtrip to work. I accepted that and supported him in his commitment to his work. But then I always knew he'd be coming back. Now the aloneness wrecked me every morning.

I have never lost a parent—mine are very much alive and lovingly involved in my life—so I didn't know what to expect from my two children, who were now adapting to life without their Dad. Josh had worked so much throughout their lives that they were used to him not being home for dinner or taking them to practices and such. However, as the weekend approached, the absence of his voice became deafening. The kids and I decided to make it a priority to do something family-oriented every weekend, or at least most weekends. Activities would range from playing a board game together, sharing a meal, going bowling or hiking, or just taking a walk around the block.

I was pretty sure that Justin and Carter would navigate this period of their lives pretty well, but I had no idea what to prepare for. Justin would cry at night as he thought about his Daddy, and I would just wrap him up in my arms and love him. Carter would cry some nights. Sometimes he'd wake up and come to me. Sleep was a bit elusive for me, and I became exhausted from managing his sleeplessness as well as my own.

Josh and I had allowed Justin and Carter to sleep together in the same room on weekends. It had become a treat for the brothers to share this time together. I decided early on that Carter and Justin could do that every night, so on one of those sleepless nights, I suggested to Carter that he sleep in Justin's room. He would pull out a comforter and blanket and sleep on the floor. My body would ache just watching him sleep on the hard, albeit carpeted, floor. But he never seemed to mind it, and it gave me such peace to see the two of them share a room and rest with each other.

The boys have always had a special bond. It would bring me to tears sometimes to see them lovingly interact with each other, especially during that time. Please don't misunderstand. There were many other instances when one was mad at the other for not listening or playing with a particular toy. But for this season, they were beautifully gentle with each other.

My brain was trying to gear up for my new status. The full weight of reality refused to settle into my mind. For a really long time, I coped by imagining that Josh was at his office. He had told each boy to imagine that he was on an extended vacation. They both thought about Josh that way, and it continued for many months. We knew he was physically gone, but our hearts refused to let go of the feeling that he was still with us. Every night when we prayed and shed tears together over our incredible loss, we would talk about Josh residing in our hearts, and how he would always be there until we met him again in heaven. It was such a comfort to think of him with us that way.

Throughout all of this, I was surprised I wasn't experiencing any real anger. I wasn't sure if it would come later. I mean, that's supposed to happen, right? That's the second of the "grief steps." I had this preconceived notion that I was supposed to be holed up in a corner, incoherent and nonfunctional. I found that, amidst the intense sense of loss, I was still getting out of bed every morning, functioning, and finding moments to be grateful and smile. It was a grayer shade of my sunnier self, but I was able to do it. I realized that oddly similar to pregnancy, any symptom you might have is considered "normal"—both normal and unique to your own experience and life's journey.

As I share this, I realize that it sounds very Zen and might not be relatable to some. But this was my experience, and I found that my faith made my journey through grief incredibly less

95

burdensome. That's not to say it didn't hurt. It was excruciatingly painful, and at some moments barely survivable. But it wasn't *every* moment. I was still able to see beauty in the shattered reality of our new life. It gave me hope and the belief that He had a purpose for all of us. I found myself trusting God and His infinite wisdom.

Monday, May 16

Anger finally came to me the Monday after his death.

I own very few dresses, and I needed something to wear at Josh's service. I also needed a respite from the house. So I asked a friend to go shopping with me in Towson so I could find something pretty to wear.

I tried on a number of dresses—anything but black or dark colors. I was fortunate to find something in a pale peach that fit my slender frame perfectly. But my friend, who struggles with weight issues, had a difficult time finding something that fit her well. As we made our way to the food court, she commented that she was glad that her husband found her attractive just the way she was. At that very moment, my sympathy for her ran out. I couldn't believe that she would choose this of all times to focus on her own insecurities. I knew she was only trying to make herself feel better, but I got mad. How could she be so selfish when I no longer had a husband to tell me he loved me and found me attractive?

I have spent my life pleasing others and trying not to rock the boat. But at that moment, I was done. I was over it. People pleasing be gone! Unfortunately, the people pleaser in me would return. But, for that brief moment, I spoke up and voiced my anger. I let her know how I felt, and she apologized.

I was thankful that Josh's service was scheduled for the following weekend. I needed time to decompress as well as prepare a beautiful Celebration of Life service for him. I was extremely surprised by how much the church takes care of funerals. I remember when I married Josh how much time and thought went into every minute detail. When I met with Pastor Brian to work out details, he said the church handled all the food.

I knew I also wanted to invite people back to the house afterward and arranged to have that food catered. As cooking is not my wheelhouse, I am always more than willing to delegate (aka pay) someone else to take on that responsibility.

A few days before the service, I took the boys shopping for some suitable dress clothes for the service. They are active-wear kids, so you can imagine the struggle I had getting them to try on dress shirts and pants. But there we were in the middle of Kohl's fitting room, figuring out what was going to work. As I was tugging at Justin's shirt, Carter decided to go body surfing on the floor on his belly, wearing the new and unpaid-for clothes. *Seriously?* Here I was trying to wrap my head around finding clothes for my boys to wear for their father's funeral, and Carter was body surfing.... So, what did I do? I broke out in laughter. It was all so ridiculous. I couldn't stop laughing at the crazy kid who was definitely not following proper fitting-room behavior. But, at that moment, I didn't care. I was so happy to smile at this silly 8-year-old who, in a single moment, lifted a magnitude of seriousness and sorrow from our lives by sliding across a dusty floor.

Late in the week, Josh's college friend Larry, whose wife had given birth just a few days after Josh died, called to say he was coming to the Celebration of Life service. In a flow of tears, I didn't argue and allowed him to show his love for Josh by coming to pay his respects. I was so grateful to his wife for supporting his decision to come.

In those weeks after Josh's death, we were inundated with flowers, cards, food, and love. It was humbling. What had we done to make so many people care? I knew that Josh and I had often focused on helping others, but it was overwhelming and absolutely incredible to feel so completely wrapped up in love.

Saturday, May 21

On the day of his service, Josh's friends from high school initiated a run in his honor. We met on a rainy morning to run two miles near the Susquehanna River. Old friends and new friends came to plod along the rain-soaked trail, all the while reminiscing about Josh and communing together. That morning, I met one of his first loves—Mandy—a beautiful soul who was his friend through high school. She pulled me aside from our group and gave me a huge hug. She tearfully told me how Josh had been such a huge help to her during the very awkward years of high school. It was just one more memory of a kindness Josh had given to another person.

My dear friends Kari, Eliza, Wendy, and Erica accompanied me to the church with my babies in tow. It was so weird, getting all dressed up and heading out. Looking sharp in their Sunday-best duds, the boys and I made our way to our non-denominational church to take part in a service to sum-up my husband's life. How do you do that in an hour? Not possible.

I stood by myself and welcomed the countless guests. I felt strong at that moment, cloaked in my new soft coral dress and standing tall in my pumps. I was ready to welcome the long line of people who had taken the time to come and honor Josh and our family. I didn't shed a tear—until I looked up and saw a small army of men in suits. I hadn't seen many of them since college, but I knew them instantly. I remembered countless crazy nights with them. They were Josh's fraternity brothers. They had played a part in introducing me to Josh and had always treated me like a sister.

When Josh enrolled at Cornell in the fall of 1994, he struggled to fit in. After winter break, he decided to try pledging a fraternity in hopes of making a connection. He met the brothers of Delta Phi and enjoyed the way they made him feel like he belonged. Still unsure, he started thinking of changing schools. One day, he was walking to the main campus to mail an application to Brown University when one of the brothers stopped him and invited him to bid night at the house. He went and found what he was looking for—a sense of belonging and acceptance by a group of crazy but lovable guys.

Later that year, I met him while he was out promoting a so-called "Hurricane Party" that the fraternity was hosting, and my friends and I soon became frequent flyers to the house. Those guys accepted me graciously among them. I felt more at home at that fraternity than I did at my sorority. Josh and I both had been searching for a sense of belonging, and the brotherhood gave both of us that gift as we entered into adulthood. So, when I looked up and saw these men before me, waiting to pay their respects to Josh and me, the tears came. I still loved those guys. Even after so many years had passed, it didn't matter. We all embraced, and they promised to come to the house after the funeral so we could all download.

As we prepared to go into the sanctuary, I saw Justin and Carter playing hide-and-go-seek with their friends. It seemed entirely inappropriate but was, in fact, a relief to me. I loved seeing them being boys and not letting every moment be clouded by the burden of their loss. It was inspiring—even though the mom in me was *appalled*. I was given a box of tissues to use as we were ushered to the front row with our families. I didn't know how I would react, but I wanted to be prepared.

Pastor Brian launched into Josh's amazing journey and his discovery of faith that conveyed a beautiful message of hope. I sat there, surrounded by nearly 400 friends, family, and my two precious boys, listening to Pastor Brian describe an incredible man: A man to whom I'd been married for nearly 15 years; a man who wanted the boys and me to be happy; a man who worked too hard at times but always did the best that he could; a man who shared his brilliant mind with friends and family; a man who wasn't perfect but loved unconditionally. That was my husband, and for two decades we had been connected. Even though saying goodbye was not on my radar yet, I felt such peace to have been in the presence of such an incredible soul.

A short video was played, a portion of the one my brother, Dave, had shot of Josh, describing his thoughts on life and his family. It was comforting but slightly disconcerting to see his happy, handsome face on the screen. But there he was, sharing that his favorite movie was *The Incredibles* and his favorite song was "Enter Sandman" by Metallica. It softened my heart as his face lit up when he described how he felt about his bride and how proud he was of me.

I hadn't always felt that he was proud of the business I had created. We'd had many discussions about how much money everything cost. But, there he was, his face glowing with love in admiration of me. I cried and missed him deeply. Surprisingly, though, I did not use the entire box of tissues. I was terrified to turn around during the ceremony to see other people grieving for Josh. It would have been too much to bear to witness their grief, too. Instead, I chose to hug my boys close to me and be proud to have had Joshua Andrew Lindenmuth as my husband.

Later, I again stood by myself at the lovely reception the church held afterward, greeting and talking to all of the people who had come out to support our family. At one point, a woman I barely knew came up to me, tearfully explaining that she wasn't sure she should have come. She shared that she had been struggling in her life and had felt compelled to join us for Josh's service. She was inspired by the message of Josh's journey and the hope that stirred her heart after hearing his story. I reassured her that she was meant to be there, and I was so happy to hear that Josh's story had given her something that she needed at that moment in her life.

I felt a deep sense of peace and connectedness to God that day. I knew He was wrapping me up in his strength and presence, and I was able to take on that day with grace, composure, and wonderment. It was weird, in a way. It was a far cry from what I had expected. I didn't know any young widows that I was close to. My only examples of what to expect were what I had seen in the movies or on TV, where the bereft, widowed spouse would go woodenly through the motions of life for months or years to come. I didn't feel bereft to the point of non-functioning. It certainly helped that I was surrounded by incredible family and friends, who kept filling me with love the whole time.

That night, I hosted an after-party to have close friends and family gather in a more intimate setting, where we could reconnect and grieve for Josh. Dozens of people came over to do just that.

I put his portrait on the kitchen counter. The mood was mostly upbeat. Pastor Brian had set the tone for our grief for the rest of the day. He had shared a message of hope amidst the loss of a dear man. We all knew that Josh wouldn't want us sitting in a stupor, crying and being utterly miserable. Instead, I heard conversations of silly antics Josh had pulled in high school and college. There were tears, but smiles as well, as people recalled how Josh always made everyone feel happy.

It had rained all day, so we couldn't go outside. Many of us communed in the garage and downstairs. It was an incredible treat to have Josh's fraternity brothers there. Justin and Carter were grateful that some of their friends made it over, and they happily played around the house with Nerf guns. Even though it was a bit chaotic, we reconnected as if no time at all had passed since we were last together.

I had arranged for the boys to go home with my parents that night. When it was time for them to leave, Justin clung to me. It was getting late, and I knew that with so many people around, the house would be loud with voices for quite a while longer. I was torn. I knew my baby needed me to hold him, but I also wanted to engage with people that loved Josh. When I'm wearing my mom hat, it's difficult to have an adult conversation for any length of time. I knew that my parents would love on the boys and provide a quiet house for them to rest. Even though my reasons were valid, my heart was heavy as I reiterated that he had to go his Nana's house. I promised to call him later and told them I loved them both, so very, very much. My parents graciously took them. I was heavy-hearted for a bit, as I tried to shake off my guilt.

All of us moms have felt the mommy guilt. It starts from the moment you find out you're pregnant. We question if we had too much to drink before we knew we were pregnant, if we're drinking too much caffeine, or if the chemicals in our hair dye will affect the unborn baby. It continues from there.

I was used to the mommy-guilt feeling, but it felt heavier that day, knowing that my babies had just lost their Daddy. I had never been a widowed parent before. I wanted to pour into them, but I also needed to guard my own sanity so I could take proper care of them. I would always give my patients the analogy of being on an airplane when wrestling with this consideration. When you're on an airplane, and the attendants explain the safety instructions, who is supposed to get the oxygen mask first when the cabin pressure drops? You or the child next to you? Answer: You, because if you pass out, you can't help anyone else. I kept this thought in mind as I gauged what I needed to do in order to function and capably tend to my children.

One of Josh's best friends from college, Matt, was the last to leave that night. He and I sat and talked and grieved together, as we processed Josh's death. Matt had always been one to joke around when he was stressed or didn't know what to say. But, that evening, he set aside the jokes to fully share and talk about Josh. They had been roommates in college and had engaged in many silly shenanigans back then. I was privy to many of their crazy stories. It was so comforting to be talking with someone who had known Josh for over two decades and had loved him dearly—and wasn't afraid to good-naturedly pick on him a little.

I think it's natural for us to honor the dead by sharing stories of how amazing they were. But remembering only their strengths puts them on a pedestal, and in our mind's eye, we raise them to a state of almost superhuman perfection. Josh was an incredible man, but he was also a man that made mistakes. With Matt, I could talk about Josh as he really was. It made me feel closer to the real man who was once my husband.

With the boys gone for the night, I insisted that Erica, Eliza, Kari, and Wendy, stay over with me. I wasn't ready for the quiet of a big house. They stayed until late morning the next day. We ate cookies for breakfast, laughing and light-heartedly teasing each other. These women are so special to me. They intuitively knew what I needed and gave it to me. They didn't mope around crying but celebrated Josh's life by being with me and embracing the joy that his life had brought to this world. It was a wonderful morning of continued connection and bonding.

My parents came by later to drop off the boys and pick up my friend, Wendy. I was still not ready to be in the house by myself, so I was grateful to have my young children to focus on. They helped me escape the magnitude of my loss, even if just for a little while.

Monday, May 23

I love taking care of people, and I wanted to do something productive. So that Monday, after two weeks away, I went back to work. My team was incredible. They didn't coddle me, and neither did they bother me with day-to-day issues. They scheduled my patients, and I went to work with them. I did my best to focus and not let my thoughts wander into the depths of my despair.

That first morning was hard. The boys had gone off to school, happy to return to a normal schedule. But I wasn't shaking off the heaviness of grief. It followed me while I listened to my patients' concerns and adjusted them. Around 11 a.m., I stepped into another room and discovered my father—my dear, loving father, with whom I share a deep connection. He and I have similar personalities. We both want to help others and try to anticipate when someone needs a hug. I started to cry and felt relief walking into his embrace. I was overwhelmed. All of my feelings rose to the surface, and I was able to release some of the weight I was carrying. For that moment, I could be my Daddy's little girl again and let him lift some of my load. "Dad, how did you know? This day is so hard. I'm *so glad* to see you!" I don't know who felt better, him or me. He couldn't take my pain away, but he was all too happy to shoulder a bit of my burden, knowing that it helped me.

Mornings continued to be hard. I would wake up every day and cry as, once again, the incredibly harsh reality of my loss set in. I would feel the magnitude of my aloneness until the kids woke up and started running around the house—breaking both the silence and the solitude.

One morning, while running with my dear friend Shannon, she asked if the annual crab feast we always held together over Memorial Day weekend could include another family. I stopped short. Suddenly, I couldn't breathe. Grief knocked the wind out of me, and I burst into tears. For the past four years, we had always gotten together, our brood and hers. In that very instant, I realized for the first time that my social life with other couples and families was going to be irrevocably different. I hadn't been prepared for that. First of all, I didn't want to do anything different and wanted to carry on the same tradition the way we always had. It had only been two weeks since Josh had died, and I just wasn't capable of handling any more changes. I had dealt with so many already, I just couldn't take any more. I especially didn't want to face the harsh reality that I was now a "single mom." Just saying it felt like stumbling through a foreign language.

Shannon thought she'd asked an innocent question and was horrified to have triggered such a reaction from me. But it was too much, and much too soon. She said, of course, we could do it, just as we had in past years, and only have our two families. I was thankful, also, to not have to meet new people. I have always been a very social person, but that part of me had been subsumed, at least for the time being, while I processed my loss.

All of my closest friends were happily married with children. No one was single, let alone widowed. I realized that now I was going to be a third-wheel when hanging out with my friends and their husbands. I had been to many social outings on my own in the past, but then Josh had been associated with me. I hadn't considered that, all of a sudden, I would be thrust into single mom-ness. That was one more club I hadn't asked to be part of.

I really started to resent it when people would come up to me and give me that pitiful look. You know, the one where they just feel sorry for you because you had just lost your "person." I never wanted pity, ever. I was grieving and appreciated support, but not depressing pity. It didn't serve my needs. Yes, I had just endured the hardest year of my life and had lost my best friend, but I didn't need to be reminded of my devastation by looking into someone's pity-oozing face.

Within two weeks of Josh's death, I called Olivia's House, a local non-profit organization that helps bereaved children. I wanted to enroll my boys into their eight-week Hearts Can Heal program, but first I wanted to know what it focused on. As I interviewed one of the program facilitators, I made it clear that I had no desire to engage in a pity party for myself or my kids. To my tremendous relief, she assured me, "We don't let anyone wear their victim coat here." Thank God! I couldn't bear the thought of sitting and wallowing in my grief with others. I signed them up for the following fall.

Monday, May 30

Memorial Day came around, and I took my children to watch my parents take part in their hometown parade in Westminster, Maryland. I sat on the sidewalk, surprised by how normally the day was progressing, and how wrong it felt. I shouldn't be sitting on this sidewalk, acting as if I hadn't just experienced the greatest loss of my life. My brother, Dave, and his family showed up and distracted me from my sadness for a while.

But when we got back to my parents' house, it hit me. The tsunami of emotion I'd been successfully keeping under wraps unleashed itself, and I raced to the backyard to cry by myself. It all felt wrong. Josh was supposed to be enjoying this day with us. He should be relaxing and playing with the boys, not gone... forever. While I sat on the Trex steps on the back deck sobbing, Dave came outside to sit with me and put his arm around my depleted shoulders. He and I had lost only grandparents and weren't equipped to deal with the magnitude of losing someone so young and close to us. But even though he was at a loss as to what to say, he sat with me as I released more of the grief and lightened my load by a minuscule amount. And, as always, the tears eventually subsided. I took a deep breath and was ready to move forward with the day. I enjoyed some more time with my family, then the boys and I left in time to head over to Shannon's house for our crab feast.

Shannon, her husband, Ryan, and I enjoyed a nice visit. Our four children were having a great time in their pool. With the kids entertained, we relaxed in the screened-in wooden gazebo and talked about Josh. I loved talking about him. It made me feel that his physical presence was close and he was very much alive.

Ryan had lost his Dad as a teenager, and he shared his experience growing up without him, and how his Mom had adapted to the role of a single mom. It had been hard for her, and she never maintained a close relationship with her late husband's family. I knew in my heart that I wouldn't let that happen with my in-laws. We had been in each other's lives for two decades, and I did not want that to change.

Then Ryan mentioned that his Mom had never remarried. It seemed really weird to be broaching the topic of remarriage so soon after my husband had passed. But I met it head-on. Josh had confided in his family members that he knew I would start dating again, that it might not be very long, and not to be upset with me.

Josh always wanted me to be happy, and he had commented many times over the years that if I would be happier finding someone new, he would support that. I always thought that he was crazy and utterly selfless. There was no question I would be with him and only him. But he was committed to my happiness. He even joked that I might meet someone at his funeral. I was glad he could be so cavalier about it, but it was nowhere on my radar. Although Josh was no longer alive, I still felt very much married to him. However, I shared with them that I had a sense that I wouldn't be alone forever. I told them that even Carter had asked me three days after Josh died when was I going to get married again. In his young mind, all of his friends were supposed to have moms and dads, and I was supposed to have a husband.

CHAPTER 9

Single Mom-ness

The first weekend in June introduced me to vacationing as a single parent. A dear friend had offered her beach house to us, and we set off for Fenwick Island, Delaware. I had gone on countless day trips with the kids without Josh, but this was the first trip to the beach without him.

I settled on the sand that evening and watched the boys as they frolicked in the water, thoroughly engaged in the moment. That profound heaviness of grief came upon me as I sat alone crying and missing my beloved. The hurt lapped at my mind like flickers of fire, mesmerizing and painful. I sat with it...for a while. But as the sun set, I'd had enough of sitting in the grief and rounded-up the boys to head back to the house.

The week before, I had received a phone call to pick up Josh's ashes from the funeral home. My parents happened to visit one afternoon, and I asked them to go with me. I had never seen human ashes before, and I was unsure of how I would react. They waited in the car while I signed the release. I was surprised how heavy the bag of ashes was. I knew I didn't want to hang on to it for long.

Years before, Josh had joked that if he passed away, I should spread his ashes in the water or anywhere I saw fit. I thought the ocean was a perfect place. Water touches the whole world, and I felt that symbolically it allowed him to be everywhere, so we would never be apart. On a cloudless afternoon, our last day at the beach, I brought out three baggies filled with some of his ashes. I hung on to some to disperse later in a few other places that had been important to us. I gave each child a bag of khaki-colored ashes, and we slowly released them into the ocean. They quickly disappeared into the salt water. The boys were somber as they released the contents, but they swiftly regained interest in playing and splashing in the water. Their urge to be carefree gave us all a respite from the seriousness of our situation. I sat on a nearby rock to watch them.

Then, Justin sidled over to talk to me.

"Are you okay, Mom?"

"I will be. It's just really hard at times." I paused. "You know, Justin, you don't have to take care of me." He seemed to have been more protective of me since Josh had passed, often asking me how I was and trying to help me around the house.

"I know Mom, but I feel like I should."

"Did someone tell you to? Did Dad?"

"No, I just feel like I should."

I was so proud of his strong, little heart but sad that, at the young age of 11, he was already feeling a responsibility to be the man of the house. I was reflecting on how much he had grown up this past year since his Dad got sick. I was in that head space when he suddenly held up his foot.

"Mom, can you help me put my sock back on?" I laughed, assured for the moment that he was still my little boy who needed my help.

After our weekend getaway, we returned home to try on our newest normal. It was like putting on ill-fitting underwear. Things get bunched in awkward places and stretched in others. But try we did. I returned to work that week and focused on treating my patients, while the boys finished their last week of school. As we muddled through that week, I started thinking about what to do with Josh's old car. It was an electric blue Saturn Ion with manual transmission and well over 200,000 miles on it. I thought it might be a good idea to hang on to it to teach the kids how to drive a stick shift. But it soon became evident that I was not going to drive the car often, and the brakes had started to lock up after sitting unused for weeks at a time. It finally dawned on me that I wanted to get rid of it. Cars were not important to Josh. In his mind they were only needed to get from point A to point B, and who cared what they looked like? I drove a 2012 base model Ford Explorer with front-wheel drive. I started dreaming about a new model with four-wheel drive and other added features.

I've mentioned before that my husband was frugal, and because of that, I was in a financial position to think realistically about getting a new car. I ventured out to the local Ford dealer to check out a Limited Edition. I barely felt worthy enough to climb into it. It felt so opulent! We had always bought base-model vehicles with minimal add-ons. I took one out for a test drive and noticed all the fancy options, such as lane assist and air-conditioned seats. I hated to think what the price tag would be for such an elaborate mode of transportation. What would Josh think? He would be horrified to know I'd even consider spending so much money on something that you just "drove."

When we bought our Explorer nearly five years earlier, we first had many discussions about it. Josh was intensely uncomfortable about having such a gas guzzler—he liked 30-plus miles-per-gallon, not fewer than 20—and it sickened him to think about what it cost, even though we certainly had the money to pay for it. Moreover, it would be a great car to transport the kids, their friends, and all their sports gear. After months of discussion, he finally agreed to it. So, with these memories seared into my mind, I felt uncomfortable making a decision I knew he would have vetoed.

Next, I test drove the Sport version, a ruby-red metallic beauty with bad-ass wheel rims. As soon as I felt the sport suspension, opened the dual sunroofs, and luxuriated in its black leather seats with red stitching, I knew I had found my car. With the encouragement of my parents, I did it. I traded in both of the older vehicles and became the proud owner of a fully-loaded SUV. The extravagance was overwhelming, and so was the guilt, knowing how Josh would have reacted. And yet, I knew in my heart that, where he was at that moment, he would not judge me. Justin gave me a bit of a hard time, initially. "Mom, I miss Dad's car. I liked your old one better." It added a bit to my guilt, yet I could tell he was enjoying the new SiriusXM radio...and the air-conditioned seats.

I dreamt about Josh a couple of weeks afterwards. He came to me, healthy and happy. In my dream, I confessed to buying the vehicle. I saw the smile fall from his face and I felt extreme disapproval coming from him. I woke up, sad to know I had disappointed my husband. But I quickly realized that was my own projection. I'm sure one can infer many things when analyzing one's own dreams, but I felt that message was pretty clear. I was learning how to make choices for myself without deferring to my spouse. It was completely alien to me. I felt like a young child, learning how to take those first few unsteady steps without assistance.

I hate labels. But I found that when I felt particularly overwhelmed, I would resort to using the single-mom label as an excuse for not getting something done because it was too hard to manage alone. Every time I said it, I felt like I was playing the victim card—which I was adamant I would never do. Being a single mom is hard, but we can do it, and we don't need to wear our single mom-ness as a label to get sympathy from people who are not in that category. We all have challenges in our lives, *all of us*. No one is exempt. Where's the growth on easy street? There is none.

With summer almost upon us, I felt that it was important for the boys to start meeting with a therapist. Even though they seemed to be doing well most of the time, Justin continued to cry most nights at bedtime. Carter didn't cry quite as often, but almost. I wanted them to be well-supported, so they could grow successfully through their healing process.

I found Jen, an excellent play therapist, and the boys started seeing her weekly. She mentioned that she sometimes would counsel her young clients' parents, too. She and I hit it off instantly, and I knew I could trust her to be my counselor as well. I also began to see her weekly. I felt it was imperative that we were all well-supported so we could meet grief face-to-face and deal with it. I didn't want Justin or Carter to spend their teenage years, which would be difficult enough, repressing their grief over the loss of their Dad. Thankfully, the boys loved "Miss Jen," and they began opening up to her and expressing all the feelings they were trying to process. Consequently, they both continued to function well and enjoy life, even while intensely missing their Dad.

CHAPTER 10

"Make Straight the Way for the Lord"

One of the many gifts Josh left behind was a letter to me. He also wrote letters to the boys, his parents, and his brother. We weren't to open them until he was gone. My letter was sweet. He reminisced about many fun vacations and special intimate moments we had shared. But at the end, he wrote about God—and how he felt that God had lessened his pain and suffering through his ordeal. Then he quoted John 3:16, "For God so loved the world that he gave his one and only Son, that whoever believes in him shall not perish but have eternal life." He said that if I believed that, too, I might want to consider being baptized, as it had been an amazing experience for him in our bathtub.

I was shocked when Josh discovered his faith in God and Jesus. I really thought pigs would fly before he would make that commitment to our Maker. But the miracle occurred before he died, and an incredible peace came over him that remained with him to the end.

I'd been baptized at the age of six months, in my grandparents' church in Ithaca, New York. Obviously, having no memory of the experience, I realized that I, too, wanted to embark consciously on the journey and experience what Josh had.

Our church in York makes a big deal out of baptisms. They

set up a large pool in the auditorium for that particular purpose. Usually, around a dozen people have their story of salvation read to the congregation one-by-one, while Pastor Brian and Pastor Steve support and immerse each person in the water. Ironically (or was it?), my church was offering an immersion baptism ceremony in the middle of June. I knew I wanted to participate. I briefly wrote about my journey and invited my parents, my brother and his family, and Josh's parents and his brother and family.

This is how I conveyed my story:

My life wasn't bad before I made the conscious decision to follow Christ. I always had a belief in God but acknowledged Him more peripherally than centrally in my life. At the time, I had already been blessed with the American Dream. I had a healthy little boy, Justin, a fantastic husband, Josh, who loved and respected me, and wonderful family and friends. But I subconsciously knew that a void existed, a hole, a lacking of full joy. I felt like the light inside me had the dimmer switch on.

After many months of trying to conceive my second son, Carter, I distinctly remember sitting in church and, realizing that God was in charge, I prayed and turned my life over to God's control on December 10, 2006. Three weeks later I discovered I was pregnant! Fast forward a few more years, with the support of my husband, I opened my own chiropractic office and have since enjoyed growth and wonderful miracles with my precious patients.

Even though I had realized He was truly in control, I held back from diving deeper into my relationship with God and Jesus. My husband was not a believer, and I was afraid to be too far different in our faith.

My prayer was that he would find God and Jesus, and that we could explore that in our marriage.

Fast forward to last July, my husband was diagnosed with a rare and aggressive cancer. The average prognosis of life was four months. What was amazing during most of this time was Josh had few side effects from the intense chemo he was on and had little discomfort. During the ensuing ten months, he discovered a profound faith. He recognized that Jesus was his savior, and he attributed his minimal symptoms to be God's doing. In light of discovering his faith, he decided to be baptized, which we were able to do in the comfort of our home. I never thought that was possible! I remember sitting in church thinking to myself that my husband will never be joining me in full faith. Never say never. Josh discovered that his cancer gave him a precious gift. A gift that allowed him new eyes and a new heart. He prayed for Jesus to enter into his life. I was astounded and humbled by the greatness of God, who revealed Himself so profoundly to my wonderful husband.

However, on May 11, Josh went home to Jesus. My heart is rejoicing that his body is healthy and whole while still saddened by missing the love of my life. As I move through this challenging chapter in my life, I am ready to be fully engaged with Christ and to be open to His plan for our two boys and myself.

As I navigate my new 'normal' without the physical presence of my beloved husband, I have, surprisingly, experienced joy in my heart. We have been beautifully supported and loved by family and friends. I recognize that that is no accident, and I feel Jesus carrying me through this season. With His help, I am even able to find the beauty around me amidst the sadness. I acknowledge that Jesus has sent so many helpers to me during this season of my life, to lift me up and carry me. I know that I am never alone. Thanks be to God!

Angela Lindenmuth

With my family in attendance, I made my descent into the pool, surrounded by hundreds of other onlookers. Pastor Steve whispered to me, "Josh is here," while Pastor Brian's eyes shone with tears of compassion for my journey. They immersed me under water, and I rose up, filled with light and joy.

I made my way to the back room in the church to change into dry clothes. I was overwhelmed. I fell to my knees and wept, "Jesus, I am yours. I am yours. Thank you for all your blessings," was my heartfelt cry. It was powerful to release the stress of the recent months and to put my faith and burden with Him. At that moment, I felt completely connected to Spirit and was at peace. It filled me with an indescribable joy.

Later that day, in our backyard, with Josh's and my family present, we planted a beautiful red maple tree, a gift from our loving friends Ryan and Shannon, and released the rest of Josh's ashes into the ground. As I write this at my kitchen table, I can see the tree's beautiful red tips pushing upward towards the heavens as they grow.

CHAPTER 11

One Step Forward, Two Steps Back

Thursday, June 23

It was the 15th anniversary of the day I had formally committed my life to Josh. I was sitting in my office, working on my notes for patient visits, when two of my staff walked in carrying a modest but beautiful bouquet of flowers, followed by another, more elaborate, arrangement, in a robust array of colors. I read the first note—it was from my very thoughtful parents. They were thinking of me that day, so endearing and sweet. I moved on to read the note attached to larger arrangement and tears pricked my eyes. I knew that chicken scratch.

Dearest Ange,

15 years ago I made the best decision of my life. We have had so much fun together, and I truly loved every moment with you. You inspired me to be a better man, and given me comfort when I most needed it.

Love,
Hubby

He had thought ahead to order flowers and write a handwritten note.

I was undone.

The carefully constructed façade crumbled, and the tsunami of grief returned. I unleashed the tears I'd been holding in check all morning. My staff knew that it was going to be difficult, so they had shut the door behind them after depositing the flowers in my office. I let the tears flow and allowed myself to *feel*...to feel the loss and to allow myself to acknowledge that *Josh was really gone*. He wasn't going to walk in the door and tell me it was some elaborate joke. He, truly, was no longer here. It was almost too unbearable to process.

After a good 15 minutes, the sobbing came to an end, and I ventured out into the hallway to see if I had a patient waiting to care for, and I did. Thankfully, it was a dear friend who was very familiar with the grief that cancer entails. He had lost a young brother-in-law the year before to melanoma. After I adjusted him, I realized I wouldn't be able to handle any more patients that day. McKenzie, my front desk manager, had known it before I did. "Dr. Sam is good to take care of the rest of your patients today." Dr. Sam, who had finally joined our practice, was more than happy to care for my patients so I could process another difficult day. And just like that, I was dismissed. I agreed I would be gone through lunch but said I might return in the afternoon.

I drove home in a daze, feeling the surges of grief come through. When I got home, I called my friend Troy to unload a bit of my mental anguish. He, too, gave me permission to take off from work. So I released the guilt of playing hooky and gave in to the day. I felt compelled to go to the park near our house and journal. We had recently installed an aluminum bench there in Josh's honor. The plaque reads, "In Loving Memory, Josh Lindenmuth— Beloved husband, father, son, brother, friend." Earlier that week, the boys and I had spread some of Josh's remaining ashes in the dirt around the legs of the bench. I felt his presence there as I enjoyed the sunny day and the beauty of the green field below.

I sat there praying and straining to hear what my heart and God were telling me.

On my way home from the park, I had an overwhelming sense that the kids and I would be spending our first Thanksgiving alone in Costa Rica. It just hit me. Both Josh's and my birthday were around Thanksgiving, and at that moment, I realized I didn't want to be in the country to celebrate our first major holiday without him. It was still five months away, but I was certain I wanted to take the boys on an adventure to honor Josh. I would plan a family trip abroad, with my two young boys, as a single mom—another first for me. It felt right and empowering. I was going to arrange it all by myself, and I couldn't wait to do my own research.

But not today. Today I wanted to stay immersed in the freedom of my unexpected day off. I decided to drive to the local Starbucks, hoping I might find a couple I know that habitually stops there for cappuccino.

I strolled into the popular hangout for business people and moms taking a break from volunteering at school and scanned the crowd. I found them, the two people in the whole world who were closest to Josh, aside from the boys and myself. I hugged them and sat down. They knew why I was there. They understood the magnitude of the day, and they knew about the flowers because they had helped Josh set it up in the first place. Elise and Zeke—Josh's parents—had worried for me about this day. They knew the flowers were going to be hard for me to deal with. But their loving smiles and warm hugs invited me in. They invited me in to share and talk about Josh.

Every day they were living in a world without their son. It was so healing to sit with the people who had brought him into the world. We shared stories about Josh, and I told them what the boys were up to. They expressed how grateful they were for the way I'd cared for Josh at the end of his life. I didn't feel I deserved the praise. I felt I hadn't done enough.

After our healing conversation, I drove to our church and found one of the pastors in his study. Pastor Brian was not in at the time, but Pastor Aaron, who was familiar with my situation, lent an ear as I shared my day with him. He ended the visit with a beautiful prayer to encourage further healing by leaning on Him through our days. By now, I was at peace with the day, and at peace in my present phase of healing.

That evening, I had the boys dress up, and we went out to a nice restaurant, a place Josh and I had frequented on previous anniversary celebrations. It felt appropriate to have Josh's offspring as my dates for dinner that night. Justin and Carter were so well behaved. They sat like little men and ate what they were served without complaint. We enjoyed a delicious dinner and turned my wedding anniversary into an event of love and completion. I thoroughly enjoyed the company of our two sons and expressed immense gratitude for them.

I was surprised by all the love I continued to feel during those weeks. It was as if God were wrapping me up in his loving arms to protect me from the full weight of loss while also showing me the beauty of love from others and of my surroundings. But, I was confused. I was still stuck thinking I was supposed to be grieving more severely, having a harder time functioning. I remember telling my therapist I wanted to make sure I was tapping into the grief and not just ignoring it. I didn't want to skip any steps during this process only to be blasted by it later in life because I had buried it, consciously or not.

I confided in her that I was not experiencing grief the way I thought I would and was concerned that I was missing something. In her immensely supportive tone and language, Miss Jen assured me that what I was experiencing was my unique journey and that taking time to reflect and grieve at times was exactly what I needed to do. She assured me I was on the right path and not missing any of the big pieces. Something else that helped me immensely during this time was the plethora of gifts Josh had left me to help me handle this chapter in my life— from letters of wisdom to financial stability. I still thank him daily.

July 4 was quickly approaching. Josh and I had agreed months before to let the boys go to computer camp at Towson University. I loved that Justin and Carter had shared an interest in computers with their Dad. Computing was not my wheelhouse, but my creative children loved to work on and create their own programs, whether it be building robotic Legos or inventing their own games on kid-friendly apps. Because I had signed them up late, the only week available for them to go was the week of July 4, which happened to start on a Monday.

Monday, July 4

That morning, I packed up the kids, and we made our way down I-83 for their first day at camp. The second we arrived, they excitedly jumped out of the car, ready to explore bits and binary functions as well as 3D printing.

My office was closed that day to observe the holiday, and I was looking forward to having a little time to myself. The reality of being a single mom meant that you don't have a partner to do the hand-off at bedtime or to help run the errands. After saying a very quick goodbye, I went to get my nails done then journal in a local Starbucks.

I started thinking about our house, and how I'd like to make some updates. Josh was amazing at so many things, but doing house projects was not at the top of his list. We still had screws in the walls the previous owners had left there twelve years before. I wanted a project that would preoccupy my attention. I was daydreaming about what changes I would like to make, and what color paint I would choose for the walls, when my Mother called. She was checking in with me and offered to pick up the boys that night, have them stay overnight, and then drive them back to camp in Towson the next day. Her generosity brought tears to my eyes. I hadn't realized how much I needed a break from being on duty, even if for only one night. I accepted gratefully and enjoyed a quiet day of solitude and reflection, while the boys happily engaged in a day of computers and machines.

Two days later, I resumed my regular routine and dropped the boys off at camp. As I was heading back to York to start my day at the office, I realized that I was driving the same route that Josh had taken back-and-forth to work a million times in the last twelve years. As I drove north on I-83, grief welled up, and gut-wrenching sobs consumed me, making it difficult to navigate the highway. And, along with the sadness, I was overpowered by a feeling of resentment that my friends and family still had their life partners with whom they could grieve. Mine was gone.

In a desperate attempt to get control of my emotions, I called my brother. He answered immediately. Dave was always at the ready during this time, ready to listen. Amazing. I choked out some words. I knew the death was hitting him hard, too. We were sharing the pain of a devastating loss neither of us had ever experienced before. He listened to my sobs and patiently let me vent my grief his way. He was so loving and gracious.

Somehow, I managed to drive safely to my office. I told my team that I was struggling that day and needed some time to collect myself. I was just overwhelmed—with grief—and by the new level of responsibility that was all on me as a mom. By trying to lead my team in my office. By trying to keep my house together. By trying to keep the kids on a routine. By trying to figure out widowhood. By trying to acknowledge my grief and let the sadness come without barricading the emotions. They needed to come out. I didn't want to squelch something this big. Such emotions need to be released!

As my waves of grief dropped from tsunami grade to 5-foot swells, I was able to breathe. I was able to focus on the here and now. I had patients to care for, so I got back to work. An hour later, my brother surprised me. He'd brought his laptop so he could work in one of our vacant rooms while I finished my morning duties. He stayed by my side, supporting me through one of my hardest days. We rounded out the evening talking over dinner at a favorite nearby restaurant. I was so grateful to his wife, Lauren, for supporting his decision to come up and help me that awful day.

The following week marked our annual trip to Deep Creek Lake in Western Maryland. I was looking forward to disconnecting from the crazy day-to-day life with the kids and spending time with my parents and my brother and his family. I packed up my new wheels and loaded in the boys.

When we arrived, my parents took us out to dinner, followed by an indulgent trip to the ice cream shop. I sat in the driver's seat while my parents and the children went into the creamery. I sat there, frozen in place with the flow of tears in full force, recalling that nearly a year ago that day, I had been with Josh, supporting him through his surgery. The heartache I'd felt since May 11 intensified. I mourned my husband and the lost reality of our family of four.

My Mother, in tune to my distress, came out to cheer me up. But I didn't want to be cheered up. I wanted to sit with it in solitude. She tried to relate to me by sharing the sorrow she felt when her parents died. I knew she was trying to show empathy and compassion, but her experiences of grief were vastly different from mine. You expect your parents to die someday, not your 40-year-old husband in the prime of life. I knew she loved me and was only trying to help. But right then, there was no one who could comfort me, not even her. I was utterly alone. Only time would help me grasp, help me absorb, what had happened to my husband. Meanwhile, I needed space to comprehend my new reality.

My brother, his wife, Lauren, and their four beautiful girls joined us at the lake the next day. It was so refreshing to be bombarded by the little ladies, as they made their energy known all over the house. They are so precious and dear. They allowed me to engage in the here and now. I got to be "Aunt Ange" to Eva (6), Skara (4), Kaiya (3), and Raina (1). Justin and Carter adore their younger cousins and reveled in the role of ringleaders to the little girls, who looked up to the older boys. That first night, as Dave and Lauren prepared a delicious Paleo dinner, we set the tables—one for the adults and one for the kiddos. It sounded good in theory, but, inevitably, one little one or another would end up at the adult table.

I sat down to a table with six chairs and saw the empty seat next to me, where Josh should have been sitting, knowing that it would never again be filled by my husband. I held it in until after dinner, then I sat alone for a while, finding solace in the relative quiet. I always felt that giving myself space to grieve would be healthy and healing for me. So when the grief started to overwhelm me, I would accept it and let it unfold entirely.

Throughout the week, among many other activities, we had water-skied and gone tubing. It was incredible to go out in the early evening on the rented ski boat and cut my slalom ski through the flat water. Later we indulged in making s'mores over the fire. I was grateful for such beautiful moments.

Later that week, I overheard my nieces yelling excitedly, trying to get my brother's attention: "Daddy! Daddy! Daddy, look!" they shouted. "Daddy"—a word I suddenly realized my boys could never utter again to their own father.

I spent some early mornings on the dock, drinking in the beauty of the days and journaling about all the feelings that came to me:

7/11/16

It's been 61 days since Josh's physical presence left this Earth. The kids and I are at Deep Creek Lake with my parents and Dave's crew. I miss him. He should be here but apparently not. It is so hard to see the empty chair and the empty space beside me in bed. I want to imagine Josh's exquisite soul in a profoundly magical place that my humanness cannot fully fathom. What comfort, but still selfish sorrow for me. But I need to embrace that sorrow so that I can heal. A lone skier just went by, delighting in the beautiful calm of the lake. The sun is so bright reflecting off the lake – so amazing. I imagine Josh in that brightness, full of love, though in a place that I can't see or encounter yet. The water is so calming. It brings me peace in my soul. I want to be able to return all the love and support people have shown me—but I don't think it works that way. I embrace and absorb it and use that as a compass—a beacon for self and others moving forward. What is my path? How do I raise my children?

7/13/2016
The beginning of vacation was emotional. I want to be one with the flow and harmony of life. Tapped into the fabric. I still feel tired—a heaviness—might be the lack of motivation on vacation. My brain feels heavy and sleepy. My mind has a lethargy to it. Josh was always the super smart one. I had once thought that I was, but I lost that sense in the shadow of his brain power. How superficial of me, but it is how I felt.

I have to remind myself that God created me for a purpose and gave me my own set of gifts. It is not a competition. It bothers me when I feel intellectually inferior, and I don't want my boys to run circles around me. I want to tap into my wisdom. I feel so many are better than me, better servants to others, prettier, smarter, more selfless. Intellectually, I know we all have our unique gifts. But what are mine?

7/16/16
I had a dream Josh was alive, bald but strong. He'd been away for two weeks to heal. He was disappointed in my choice to buy the car. I resented his judging my choices. When I woke up, I realized Josh loves me and would be so happy to be reunited if he were alive. I realized that his spirit is in such a beautiful place that I can't imagine he would want to come back. I wouldn't want to take away that precious gift from him. I am head of my family now. It's me. It scares me a bit. Want to be wise and mindful of my choices....One day at a time....

Now that I was head of my household, I was starting to make decisions about our family finances—where and when purchases should be made. I was used to discussing these things with Josh. He'd had his own ideas about money and where to spend it and when, which had influenced nearly all of my buying decisions.

I was only just beginning to realize that I was now entirely in charge. I knew in my heart that Josh would want me to be happy and to spend or not spend as I saw fit. But it was such a new concept for me. I had always deferred to him. Even in death, I didn't want to dishonor him or do what something I knew he wouldn't want me to do.

But he wasn't here anymore. And I was.

CHAPTER 12

Finding My Voice

On the 71st day after Josh's death, I made a pivotal decision. I took off my wedding rings. I had been debating what to do about them. I even Googled about it. (I was horrified by the black Death Rings that were being sold to honor a deceased loved one and instantly knew that kind of commemorative symbolism was not right for me!)

One night, I tried putting my rings on my right hand, but it's slightly larger, and they became uncomfortable. But, I wanted to move forward with life. I had to let go of being Josh's wife and transform into a woman who was mourning her late husband. So, on that 71st day, I boldly took my rings off and put them in my pocket. My message was clear. I was no longer married. I was my own woman who was capable of making her own wise decisions. I also made clear my feeling for my late husband by wearing his wedding band on my right middle finger, where it fit perfectly.

I have found there is no right or wrong answer to this dilemma. I had a friend who took her rings off immediately following her husband's death. I'd known others who continued to wear them until the day they died. I was surprised by the array of emotions that overtook me once I'd made the decision. I felt that, as long as I had my rings on, they'd symbolize that I was still looking over my shoulder. I'd either be hoping that Josh would be proud of my decisions or worrying that he'd disagree. I had never been in a position before where I could make decisions for myself. I had been left here to figure out life on my own.

Josh was gifted in many ways, but he was firm in his ideas. I could never win an argument with him, so long ago I'd decided that backing down was easier. Please don't misunderstand this for complacency or giving up who I was. But believe me, I picked my battles carefully. I was ready now to venture out and let my own thoughts, opinions, and ideas guide me. I was no longer Josh's wife, one-half of a team that had worked to create a life together. That team no longer existed. I needed to figure out who Angela Renée Lindenmuth was, as a single woman.

At the end of July, the kids and I took a trip to Williamsburg with our friends Shannon and Ryan and their two children. I packed up the car and we drove down to Virginia through a thunderstorm. It was hot that weekend, but luckily their pop-up camper was air-conditioned. This was the fourth annual camping trip we had all enjoyed together. It felt off without Josh's there to round out the dynamics and fun.

One day, we decided to head over to Busch Gardens. Justin wanted to ride another roller coaster, but no one else wanted to. He kept pushing for his way. The more he pushed, the more frustrated I got. I knew Josh would have quickly diffused the situation and it would have been a non-issue. But now I was Mom *and* Dad. Josh had been more of the disciplinarian. I always wanted peace and harmony and would tend to shy away from conflicts and disagreements. Don't misunderstand me. I certainly discipline my children. But, in the past, when I really got frustrated, Josh would step in and handle the conflict. He was always good at taking the emotion out of a disagreement. To him, it was just another idea or difference of opinion, and emotions had nothing to do with it. He rarely got emotional, and when he did, it was usually for positive reasons, such as being proud of the kids or with me. With Josh's example in mind, I managed to stand my ground and tell Justin, "No." Eventually, he came around and realized his mistake. I found that taking the time to talk to my children individually allowed me to verbalize what issues were at stake and how they made others feel. Then we could work out a solution.

We finished the weekend in Colonial Williamsburg, learning how the colonial community functioned more than three hundred years ago.

Over the next ten days, I wrote the following messages in my journal:

> *8/3/16*
> *Dear Josh,*
>
> *I MISS YOU! I miss holding your hand, kissing you, talking with you, leaning on you. It's like I have a box around me, and no matter how hard I rail and scream, I can't get to you. It's been 84 days. I am learning that I don't need to do everything for your approval. I know you love me and are proud of me. You gave me so MANY blessings and gifts! I can never thank you enough. I want to honor and remember you….*
>
> *I am leaning into God/Jesus and healing—then I will ease into the next chapter.*
>
> *8/7/16*
> *Spent the night with our friends, the Goldsteins. Awesome friends. Got to talk a lot about Josh— so healing. I LOVE you, honey!!! The boys had orthodontic expanders put in three days ago. They are not enjoying it—want to be wise on how to encourage them—handle it. Food? Incentive?*
>
> *8/8/16*
> *I sit on Josh's bench contemplating money. I need to trust Him and my heart. It is so freeing to let go and release concerns. It is necessary for growth. Today I want to heal. I want to open up my office*

space for change and then use it to create—create presentations, create messages of hope, create my dreams. I was given the gifts of love, compassion, caring, and optimism. I have nothing to lose and all to gain.

8/9/16
Last night, Justin told me he was too tired to go to football. After rearranging plans and orchestrating my schedule him to get there, I was disappointed and mad. We all work hard, and sometimes we all have to do things we don't want to. I'm tired. I have no reference for being a single mom. I have no close single moms that are widows. I am in unchartered territory here. How do I fill up? Prayer, talking to Josh, asking for help? How do I grieve?

8/10/16
Yesterday was a tough day, but a beautiful person left flowers for me. I am continually being lifted up in support and love. Thank you, God! My intention today is to have patience, to breathe, and be grateful.

8/12/16
Today, I am healthy, positive, loving, giving, embracing life. I can understand why people never want to remarry. It takes a lot of commitment to be happily married. With someone else, you always have to coordinate and compromise.

I vowed I would be an open channel. I would be open to God's love and Josh's presence. I would feel my heart guiding me through a wide array of emotions, and I would embrace every single one without question or judgment. I was on this journey of life, and I wasn't going to shy away from it. Not anymore....

I had no idea what I was about to experience.

CHAPTER 13

Renewal

Saturday, August 13

Sarah, Karen's sister and one of Josh's best friends, was getting married at her parents' beautiful home on the Western Shore in Maryland. Before I started the drive down, I refused to think about how hard it might be. I had never been to a wedding by myself before. Indeed, when I got there, I found myself surrounded by couples absorbed in private conversations. I started to feel dread, so, with a glass of wine in hand, I focused on reaching out to the people I knew.

Before the ceremony began, Sarah's niece Gabby grabbed my hand and brought me to Sarah. We embraced and felt Josh's presence together. She looked so beautiful and happy! During the service, they honored Josh by mentioning his name. Tears started rushing down my face, and Kristin, one of Sarah's friends, came over to hold my hand. The ceremony, framed in the sunset, was glorious. That whole evening, I felt Josh's presence. He was there guiding others to help me when it got really hard. It was wonderful to see Chris, Sarah's new husband, looking at his new bride, completely in love, though it was excruciating to feel the loss of that love in my life. Karen was at my side the second she sensed I was really struggling. I am forever grateful! Then Sarah, the ever-thoughtful bride, had me sit next to her at the reception. I was so taken care of. I had been so sure I would leave the wedding early, but I found myself dancing and genuinely enjoying the evening.

At the end of the night, the last van waited for us until we were ready to head back to the hotel. I'd had a few drinks and just wanted to eat the leftover mac 'n cheese (it was so good)! Finally, we headed back to the hotel—a couple, myself, and the driver that night, Paul Marick, a friend of Karen's.

As Paul drove, he and I chatted about our lives. I shared Josh's story over the past year. He was very interested and a good listener. I remember enjoying the energy of our conversation and how easily it flowed. (He missed a turn– apparently, he was distracted by our discussion.)

Sunday, August 14

The next morning, at the brunch provided for the overnight wedding guests, I had time to catch up with some of Karen and Sarah's family members. As I was finishing my breakfast, Paul walked in and sat in a vacant seat right next to me. My first feeling was of complete embarrassment. I didn't remember every detail of what I said the night before—even though I was reasonably sure I hadn't said anything too outlandish. He and I quickly engaged in conversation, and I realized there was an energy between us. It scared me. I did everything I could to keep some distance between us without being too noticeable. We chatted for an hour, during which time we talked with others. I tried not to make it obvious that, really, I only wanted to talk to him. I also found myself avoiding his green eyes. They were too much to look into...so, I avoided....

After an hour of conversation, I reluctantly pulled myself away, said my goodbyes, and gave hugs—to all except Paul. I did not want to touch him or get near him, specifically because I felt something pulling me toward him—and I had no idea what to do with that!

My life was on a trajectory that was completely alien to me. It was full of endless challenges, yet, with my faith in God, they seemed surmountable. He gave me strength when I was floundering. He gave me beauty when I was struggling with my daily responsibilities. He gave me family and friends to lift me up and show me a level of compassion and love that I had never fully realized. And He gave me hope for a future that would be bright and full of new adventures with my kids. This future held love again. It also held opportunity for growth as a woman who was just starting to find her own voice.

Driving home that afternoon, I saw two white birds fly over the highway. At first, I thought they were a sign, representing Josh and me. But that didn't feel right. It was different. Then my heart stirred, and I understood. These two, beautiful white birds, that seemingly appeared out of nowhere, represented a new love that I would grow into, with someone else.

I kept thinking about Paul, and how I had this sense that somehow he was going to be in my life, in my future. I felt I was on the brink of experiencing a new love—one that would help me explore my newfound voice. It was as if Josh had led me to Paul, a man who was willing to honor me and my children and also respect my grief for the loss of my beloved. I knew I would always carry Josh in my heart, but I found that I also had room for a new love. It surprised me.

Epilogue

5/11/2017
Today marks the first anniversary of when Josh, my
love, drew his last breath and received his angel's
wings.

In the couple of weeks leading up to the first anniversary of Josh's death, my emotions decided to go on a crazy rollercoaster ride. I was not prepared for the vacillating feelings that would rock me to my core, challenging me to determine who I was and what I was truly feeling.

My heart ached for my husband. He didn't want to leave his wife and children. He didn't want to be physically away from us. Many of our last conversations had been about our children, finances, computer passwords, and his new found faith. Throughout his illness, I'd taken the best possible care of him and had always tried to maintain a positive attitude. I was happy to give that to him—to care for the man I married without letting myself dwell on the fact he was about to depart this Earth. Nor did I stop to think what my life would look like as a single mom, raising two boys.

The previous two years had brought such an enormous spectrum of emotions, from intense loss to profound joy and every shade in between. I'd been slingshotted into massive change. I'd lost the first love of my life; I'd had to figure out the new social dynamics as a widow; my children were growing up (with puberty on the horizon); I was running a business; I had embarked on a new relationship; and all the while I had been trying to maintain my sanity.

I had no idea that when I said, "I do," on June 23, 2001, that it would all change completely on May 11, 2016. I had no experience of being a widow, or a single mom, or dating at 40. But I had learned so much in my life journey with Josh. He had taught me how to be independent in ways I never thought possible. And, since his death, I have found a deeper sense of self and the voice I've always had but never thought I could express. I must say I am happy to be smiling and functional after all the changes I've been through.

I thank God for His love, and I continually thank Him for being with me through this walk in life.

> *6/13/2017*
> *Here I am, on the brink of publicly committing to another man in my life, Paul Marick. It was as if Josh and God had led me to a man who would honor my healing, my uniqueness, and my dreams, someone who would accept my children as his own. One day....*

As I prepare to blend my life with Paul and our three precious boys, Justin, Will, and Carter, I have spent time examining my goals, my intentions, and what it all means. God provided me with a life for which I felt I had no compass. But, with His help, we figure it out as we roll along, right?

Growth happens through the pain. I can never put down the words to adequately express my profound gratitude and love for Josh. We shared so much of life in our two decades together. No regrets, just a bounty of sweet memories and never-ending love in my heart for him.

Paul has given me the gift of grace and support through this new chapter in our life together. I had no idea that my heart had space to love and grieve for Josh while, at the same time, grow in life and love with Paul. It's not "either/or" when it comes to the heart...it's "and."

Gratefully, I have the support of another man, who will love me completely and honestly and give me the space to grow in the purpose God has for me. And, as I merge with another in life, I feel alive again in ways I never expected.

Acknowledgements

Josh—we shared an incredible life together—so many firsts and wonderful memories. You will always be in my heart.

Justin and Carter—our precious boys. You both have been so absolutely inspiring on this journey of life. Your Dad and I will always love you no matter where we are.

Paul—your unwavering support and love continues to astound me. You and Will have made our family whole again. I'm so grateful that Josh led us to find each other.

My parents, Bob and Linda—I've always known that you were there for me, no matter what. I'm so grateful to have such loving parents.

Josh's parents, Frank and Elise—you both are so incredible. I'm so thankful to know you both and to have a beautiful relationship with you that will continue throughout our lives.

Dave—you so graciously loved and supported me, both on the good days and the bad. Thank you for being so present throughout this journey with Josh and beyond. I couldn't ask for a better little brother.

Jake—you are so great at keeping family close to the heart. Thank you for modeling that for Josh. He always admired you for that.

Shannon—you listened to me so patiently on our countless runs as I processed this chapter of my life. I've treasured the fun times together with our families and hope for many more to come!

Karen and Sarah—Thank you for being such incredible friends to Josh and to me. You were always there, giving us exactly what we needed when we needed it.

Elaine—you heard my voice and helped me express it in a way that allowed me to share this profound journey with others.

Pam, McKenzie, Roxanne, and Sam—you kept our doors open and allowed our office to serve our members during the hardest time of my life. Thank you so very much for believing in our mission of serving and helping facilitate healing for our community.

And thank you to all of the countless, amazing people who lovingly supported and prayed for Josh and me. We felt completely wrapped in love, which made this chapter of our lives beautiful, in spite of the massive challenges that we faced. Thank you....

Printed and bound by PG in the USA

USA2019PGIL